Entertainment Weekly

COLLECTOR'S EDITION

The Ultimate Guide to THE Arrowverse

Contents

CRISIS ON INFINITE EARTHS

4
Heroes United
Inside the making of the epic five-hour television crossover event

10
Greg Berlanti: The Super Producer
He's the force behind all six heroic shows

12
Your Crossover Cheat Sheet
Trying to catch up on what happened when? We've got your back

14
Will Lightning Strike Again?
Black Lightning hasn't appeared in the Arrowverse—until now

ARROW

16
Unbroken Arrow
Here's how Oliver Queen will handle his biggest challenge yet: the series finale

28
Q&A: Stephen Amell
The star reminisces about his audition and how it felt to see the final script

32
Struck by Cupid's Arrow
Olicity fans, rejoice! In praise of the lovebirds Queen and Smoak

THE FLASH

34
Back in a Flash
Barry's the fastest man alive, and he's sure to tell you so: Meet Team Flash

42
Q&A: Grant Gustin
The actor recalls that heavy season 5 story line, plus his future hopes

46
Who's Really the Fastest?
Here's how Barry Allen actually stacks up against other speedsters

SUPERGIRL

48
The Supergirl Next Door
The Girl of Steel protects her Earth from foes alien and domestic

56
Q&A: Melissa Benoist
The actress opens up about that Lena Luthor shocker and more

60
All Dolled Up
Try on all of Kara's outfits using these paper dolls—including season 5's pants

DC'S LEGENDS OF TOMORROW

62
The Legends Are True
It's a time-travel show starring misfit heroes—what's not to love?

70
Q&A: A Super Ensemble
The cast discusses what it takes to be a Legend

78
A Not-So-Accurate Time Map
A snapshot of some of our favorite missions

BATWOMAN

80
Batwoman Begins
Cue the Bat-signal! Kate Kane has suited up—and it's about time

86
Q&A: Ruby Rose
The newest caped crusader talks about her first days on-set

BTS

90
Behind the Super Scenes
The heroic cast is caught goofing off in these fun candid photos

PREVIOUS PAGE AND ABOVE
PHOTOGRAPHS BY ART STREIBER

↑ **From left** Brandon Routh, Stephen Amell, Melissa Benoist, Grant Gustin and Caity Lotz

HeR

oes

United

SIX SHOWS. DOZENS OF SUPES. NATURALLY IT'S THE END OF THE WORLDS AS WE KNOW IT. BUCKLE UP FOR THE CW'S ANNUAL ARROWVERSE CROSSOVER.

BY CHANCELLOR AGARD ●
PHOTOGRAPH BY CARLOS SERRAO

THERE WAS NEVER SUPPOSED TO BE AN ARROWVERSE. Seriously, it wasn't planned. "A lot of people like to think we did," says Arrowverse architect Greg Berlanti. "Each step was a surprise."

When *Arrow,* the shared universe's namesake that stars Stephen Amell as the Green Arrow, premiered on the CW in 2012, the producers were repeatedly asked if they would introduce other heroes with superpowers. "The answers to all those questions were, 'No, no and no,'" says *Arrow* executive producer Marc Guggenheim. "None of those interviews have aged particularly well."

He's not wrong, because in the past eight years the CW has become the home of six DC Comics shows that exist in the same TV universe and intersect (at a minimum) on a yearly basis: *Arrow, The Flash, Supergirl, DC's Legends of Tomorrow, Black Lightning* and *Batwoman.* "If I had to pick one word, I'd say 'unbelievable,'" says Guggenheim about the universe's very existence and annual crossover events. "The truth is [the unexpected expansion] really speaks to my whole philosophy about building a universe," says Guggenheim. "The best way to do that

is to do one good show. That one is really hard," he adds. "Then if you succeed, do a second really good show." And if you produce six good shows? Well, then you attempt your most ambitious crossover yet, "Crisis on Infinite Earths," a five-hour adaptation of Marv Wolfman and George Pérez's multiverse destroying epic that rocked DC Comics in 1985 and 1986.

In a way, the road to "Crisis" began midway through *Arrow's* first season, when Berlanti started toying with the idea of bringing in the Scarlet Speedster. After talking to Warner Bros. TV and the CW, *Glee's* Grant Gustin was introduced as a pre-superspeed Barry Allen in *Arrow's* second season before headlining *The Flash,* which debuted in fall 2014.

↑ From left Curtis Holt/Mister Terrific (Echo Kellum), Amaya Jiwe/Vixen (Maisie Richardson-Sellers), Rene Ramirez/Wild Dog (Rick Gonzalez), Sara Lance/White Canary (Caity Lotz), Barry Allen/the Flash (Grant Gustin), Nate Heywood/Steel (Nick Zano), Oliver Queen/Green Arrow (Stephen Amell), Ray Palmer/The Atom (Brandon Routh), Mick Rory/Heat Wave (Dominic Purcell) and Leo Snart/Earth-X's Citizen Cold (Wentworth Miller).

Despite *Arrow's* success, the producers were worried about *The Flash* because of the special effects required to render the hero's powers. "It's famously what put the original *Flash* show out of business years ago; they couldn't get the episodes done in time," says Berlanti. But *The Flash* did work, and remains the network's highest-rated show six seasons later.

In December 2014 they attempted something even more adventurous: a two-night crossover between *Arrow* and *The Flash.* "[CW President] Mark Pedowitz was like, 'I want to cross over these two shows,'" says Guggenheim.

Who's Who on Infinite Earths

RETURNING REGULAR CAST MEMBERS ALLY WITH HEROES ACROSS MULTIPLE UNIVERSES, INCLUDING THESE HEROIC GUEST STARS. *BY ALYSSA SMITH*

Jefferson Pierce

BLACK LIGHTNING

CRESS WILLIAMS

The high school teacher and electricity-powered vigilante protects the fictional city of Freeland, alongside his two daughters—and hasn't shown up in a CW crossover yet, despite starring on the same network. Their reasoning? Different Earth. His time is finally here.

Jay Garrick/ Barry P. Allen

THE FLASH/ CRIMSON COMET

JOHN WESLEY SHIPP

Earth-3's version of the Flash has regularly helped Barry on Earth-1. Earth-90's iteration is the last known survivor of his world after the Monitor's destruction. Shipp has also portrayed Earth-1's Henry Allen—and the Flash in the 1990s show.

Kal-El and Lois Lane

CLARK KENT/ SUPERMAN

TYLER HOECHLIN AND ELIZABETH TULLOCH

Earth-38's Man of Steel keeps in contact with his cousin Kara Zor-El. During the Elseworld's crisis, he met both Earth-1's Arrow and the Flash—and after the disaster was over, he went back to propose to longtime girlfriend Lois.

Bruce Wayne

BATMAN

KEVIN CONROY

He started voicing Batman in the 1992 TV show *Batman: The Animated Series* and has continued to do so in dozens of spinoffs and video games. In "Crisis," Conroy will play an older Bruce Wayne.

Dick Grayson

ROBIN

BURT WARD

Holy nostalgia, Batman! The original Boy Wonder, who portrayed a young Grayson opposite the late, great Adam West's Bruce Wayne/Batman in the 1960s TV show and 1966 film, will play a new character in the Arrowverse.

Kal-El and Lois Lane

CLARK KENT/ SUPERMAN

TOM WELLING AND ERICA DURANCE

Somebody saaaave them! For 10 years the WB's *Smallville* followed the adventures of young Clark (and starting in season 4, Lois) before they left their small town for the big city. The two will reunite in "Crisis," playing an alternate Earth's Superman and Lois Lane.

Kal-El

CLARK KENT/ SUPERMAN

BRANDON ROUTH

Yes, there's another one. Routh has portrayed Arrowverse's Ray Palmer/The Atom for years, but his breakout role was back in 2006 in *Superman Returns*. For "Crisis," he dons a suit inspired by Alex Ross and Mark Waid's Kingdom Come.

↑ **From left** With their powers swapped during Elseworlds, the Flash (now Amell) and Arrow (now Gustin) get help from Supergirl (Benoist).

"Greg and I both grew up on *The Six Million Dollar Man* and *The Bionic Woman*. In all honesty, [those two shows] were the inspiration for the crossover."

The universe continued to expand. In 2014 now Warner Bros. president Susan Rovner met with Berlanti and company about developing a show about *Supergirl,* Superman's cousin. "I thought it was a fantastic idea," says Arrowverse EP and Berlanti Productions president Sarah Schechter. "I remember [Greg] said to me, 'I think I figured out Supergirl. It's Ginger Rogers. Ginger Rogers had to do everything Fred Astaire did but backward and in heels," says Schechter. "That really resonated [with me] as a woman working in this business."

Thus, in October 2015, *Supergirl* took flight on CBS with *Glee*'s Melissa Benoist as the titular Girl of Steel. Even though it (initially) aired on a different network, it was considered part of its CW brethren's universe because *The Flash*'s second season had established the concept of the multiverse. Toward the end of *Supergirl's* season 1, Gustin's Flash, who resides on Earth-1 with the other CW shows, zoomed over to *Supergirl* on Earth-38 for a breezy team-up. "Grant and Melissa are just so effervescent," Schechter says. "It wasn't calculated. It was a very

↑ **From top** Heroes gather after the West-Allen wedding is interrupted; Overgirl (Benoist), the evil alter ego of Supergirl from Earth-X; the Legends (and Arrow) during "Crisis on Earth-X."

pure, creative desire [of] wishing we could see them together."

At the time of *Supergirl's* launch, the producers were also developing the time-traveling drama *DC's Legends of Tomorrow,* which starred lovable screwups collected from the ranks of *Arrow* and *The Flash,* including Caity Lotz (Sara Lance/White Canary) and Brandon Routh (Ray Palmer/the Atom). Whereas the previous three series had a traditional development process, *Legends* broke the mold. They didn't even have time to make a pilot. "We literally just did clips from our other shows that we hadn't used, and we shot two days of just like, 'Wouldn't this be cool to see all of these characters onscreen at the same time?' " says Berlanti.

In 2016 *Supergirl* leaped over to the CW for its second season, further integrating into the Arrowverse via the three-part crossover "Invasion!" and a musical episode on *The Flash.* With four superheroes shows, the showrunners made a concerted effort to differentiate them all. "If you look back on that particular season that year, you'll see *Legends* became wackier, *Supergirl* went more in on aliens, *Flash* went more in on science, and *Arrow* went more in on gritty crime," says Guggenheim.

Having *Supergirl* on the CW also led to what Guggenheim calls the "gold standard" of their annual crossovers: 2017's "Crisis on Earth-X," which spanned all four shows and included two weddings, Nazi doppelgängers and more than 15 superheroes. "That was one of the craziest things I've ever done," says Benoist of appearing in a scene with every Arrowverse hero. "That particular moment is one that is going to stick with me forever, because I think we all felt it."

The Arrowverse's multiversal fight against superpowered Nazis, however, took a toll on everyone involved. "It killed all of us. We were feeling the effects of it literally a year after," says Guggenheim. "Earth-X" was so exhausting that they wanted to take 2018 off before attempting to do "Crisis"; however, the network ultimately persuaded them to do "Elseworlds" in 2018. Ironically, the topsy-turvy "Elseworlds" is the three leads' favorite one yet. "Everyone was just laughing all the time, and there was so much comedic relief to it," says Benoist. "Elseworlds" also marked Ruby Rose's *Batwoman* debut ahead of her show's 2019 launch.

All of this has been building toward the 2019 crossover: "Crisis on Infinite Earths," which will unfold across *The Flash, Supergirl, Legends, Batwoman* and the final season of *Arrow.* Chronicling a fight to save the multiverse, the Homeric tale is an ode to DC Comics' past and present as it features the return of *Smallville's* Tom Welling and Erica Durance as Clark Kent and Lois Lane, and will also introduce *Black Lightning's* Cress Williams, who has until now remained separate from the Arrowverse. Says Guggenheim: "My main goal has always been, 'How do we honor the original *Crisis on Infinite Earths?*' " I think we've crafted something really, really special." Sounds like they've got this particular crisis handled. ●

Greg Berlanti The Super Producer

A childhood fan of DC's ***CRISIS ON INFINITE EARTHS,*** the 47-year-old is now ushering the epic crossover to the small screen. BY CHANCELLOR AGARD

THE DC COMICS EVENT *CRISIS ON* *Infinite Earths* means a lot to producer Greg Berlanti.

Originally published from 1985 to 1986, *Crisis* is one of the most iconic and game-changing comic-book stories ever told. Written by Marv Wolfman and penciled by George Pérez, the 12-issue epic followed DC heroes on a mad dash to save the multiverse from imminent destruction at the hands of the Anti-Monitor. In doing so it forever changed the DC Universe ("Worlds will live. Worlds will die. And the universe will never be the same").

When it launched, *Crisis* was mainly an attempt by DC to clean up its very complicated continuity. For Berlanti, though, it was something more: It was his introduction to the wider DC pantheon, beyond just the Flash, his favorite superhero, because in those pages readers saw the younger Superman of Earth-1 interact with a graying Superman from Earth-2, the Green Lanterns' home base on Oa and so much more.

"It was a great way to get into all the characters at once because it was like a labyrinth of storytelling," Berlanti, an executive producer on all the CW's superhero shows, tells *EW*. "So you were starting to see how all of these characters were interconnected,

← The comic cover of *Crisis on Infinite Earths* (far left), published in 1985. Left: Barry Allen (Grant Gustin) discovers a newspaper dateline queuing up the crisis.

→ Berlanti in 2016.

and then that made you want to go and read the different issues that were happening and get into the different things."

The scale of the *Crisis* story drew the young Berlanti in too. "The thing that Dungeons & Dragons and *Lord of the Rings* and the DC space had at the time [in the stories they were doing] was how you got a sense of 'Oh my God, this story is bigger than all of these other little stories, [and] I can figure it out,' " he says. "There was no online community to connect with. You felt a part of it by like, 'Oh, I can get that piece of information, or I can go get that comic book or that issue, and I can fill in the blanks of being part of this bigger thing.' "

Now the time has come for Berlanti and the Arrowverse creative team to put their own spin on *Crisis.* The Arrowverse first teased the massive event way back in *The Flash*'s 2014 pilot, which ended with a shot of a newspaper revealing that the Flash (Grant Gustin) would vanish in a crisis in 2024. (Because of some timey-wimey shenanigans, that year eventually changed to 2019.) Berlanti admits that he and the other producers had no idea if they'd ever actually be able to pay that off.

"It's our iteration of it," he says. "It's not necessarily what they'd end up doing in the film space, so we could advocate for it that way, in terms of permission."

Nevertheless, this is still one of the biggest stories in comic-book history, and that is not lost on Berlanti and company. "Whenever we do an iconic story line," he says of his adaptation work, "we have a sense of pressure and obligation of 'Oh wow, we really don't want to mess this up' even more so than we usually do." He adds, "It's the closest I ever feel to being a kid again, without a doubt." •

Your Crossover Cheat S

↑ The Flash (Grant Gustin, left) and Arrow (Stephen Amell) in their very first team-up.

Heroes Join Forces

Speedster **Barry Allen** (Grant Gustin) and archery enthusiast **Oliver Queen** (Stephen Amell) spent a fair amount of time commuting between Queen's then Starling City and Allen's Central City; Allen's first cameo on *Arrow* even predated the onset of his metahuman powers. During their first official crossover, the two heroes helped defeat villains in both cities and still found time to sharpen their skills by training together. In 2015's "Heroes Join Forces," they encountered the reincarnated Hawkgirl and Hawkman, setting up a plotline for *DC's Legends of Tomorrow.*

↑ Supergirl (Melissa Benoist)

Invasion!

BARRY ACCIDENTALLY LANDED ON PARALLEL Earth-38, where **Kara Zor-El** (Melissa Benoist) makes her home, in *Supergirl's* season 1. That neatly set up Barry to introduce her to the rest of the team when an entire race of aliens called the Dominators invaded Earth-1. "I thought you were bringing an alien," says Oliver. Kara demonstrates by flying and lasering her house seal into the floor. "I'm convinced," deadpans Diggle (David Ramsey) for all of us. The action takes place over episodes in *The Flash, Arrow* and *Legends,* although there's a sweet recruitment scene in *Supergirl.*

Crisis

IT WAS A WEDDING THAT WENT WAY way, waaaay wrong. Barry and Iris (Candice Patton) try to get hitched (and invite all their superhero friends across multiple Earths while doing so), but they are interrupted at the altar by the evil versions of themselves. Yes, really. Supergirl, the Legends, Arrow and the rest face off against the SS team (led by

heet

Five crossovers, more and more superheroes and increasingly ambitious in scope: Here's everything you **NEED TO KNOW** about what happened when. BY ALYSSA SMITH

↑ Iris West (Candice Patton, center) and Barry Allen.

on Earth-X

the **Dark Arrow**, his wife, **Overgirl,** and the **Dark Flash**) in a no-holds-barred fight that leaves Legend Marty Stein (Victor Garber) mortally wounded. At the end, when all the Nazis are defeated, it's not just Barry and Iris who quietly tie the knot; Oliver and Felicity (Emily Bett Rickards) make it official as well (it took three separate proposals!).

↑ The Nazi versions of Arrow and the Reverse-Flash (Tom Cavanagh).

Elseworlds

Meet the Arrowverse's newest heroine: **Batwoman!** When the Legends don't pick up the phone (they have a disaster of their own making abrew), the life-swapped Oliver (now the Flash) and Barry (now Green Arrow) recruit assistance against the Monitor (the universe's big bad) in what turned out to be the likeliest of places: Gotham. It's their best idea ever, after first stopping to pick up a confused Kara Zor-El from Earth-38, who is the only one who realizes the heroes have exchanged lives. Eventually things go back to what passes for normal.

↑ Batwoman (Ruby Rose, top) meets a power-swapped Arrow (above).

Will Lightning Strike Again?

The electricity-powered hero **BLACK LIGHTNING** has been absent from all the Arrowverse crossovers. Here's why that's about to change. BY CHANCELLOR AGARD

***BLACK LIGHTNING* IS UNLIKE ANY** of the CW's other caped shows—and not just because of its predominantly black cast. On *The Flash* the Scarlet Speedster protects the multiverse from evildoers, and on *Supergirl* the Girl of Steel fends off extraterrestrial threats. But on *Black Lightning*—overseen by Arrowverse chief Greg Berlanti—the superhero is more concerned with mortal-world problems.

"The conflict here is not necessarily saving the world or battling aliens," Cress Williams, who stars as the electricity-powered title character, told *EW* in 2018. "It really is looking at real-life problems in an actual city, in an

↑ **Clockwise from left** Jefferson Pierce/Black Lightning (Cress Williams); Jennifer/Lightning (China Anne McClain) and Anissa/Thunder (Nafessa Williams); villain Tobias Whale (Krondon), Pierce with ex-wife Dr. Lynn Stewart (Christine Adams).

actual neighborhood and trying to conquer those problems—i.e., drugs and corruption, gun violence, police violence and just oppression that happens below the poverty line."

While it's likely *Black Lightning* has remained outside of the Arrowverse for mostly creative reasons until now, there's a second factor at play: *Black Lightning* shoots in Atlanta, and the other shows film in Vancouver, which complicates crossover logistics.

When the show begins, Black Lightning the superhero is no more. There's only Jefferson Pierce, a father who retired from crime-fighting nine years ago in order to keep his family together and now works as a teacher at a charter school. That doesn't stay the case for long. When the local One Hundred gang, led by the show's big bad Tobias Whale (Marvin "Krondon" Jones III), threatens his daughters Jennifer (China Anne McClain) and Anissa (Nafeesa Williams), he's pulled back into the game.

That focus on family also helps differentiate the drama from its network siblings. "I started out thinking family drama first," said showrunner Salim Akil. "I wanted every person—Hispanic, white, black, Asian, whoever you are—to be able to recognize yourself."

The drama wastes no time at all in bringing the Pierce family into the superhero action. Halfway through the show's first season, Jefferson's daughter Anissa discovered she had superstrength and became TV's first black lesbian superhero in the process. "I'm just really grateful to tell the story for young lesbians—and black lesbians in particular—who don't really see themselves on TV," said Williams, who cried the first time she wore her Thunder costume. "It was so freaking emotional." It was just the beginning, as sis Jennifer also gained powers in season 1.

Black Lightning also stands out from other superhero shows because it uses the black American experience to inform its story. Jefferson, as well as the metahumans we meet in season 2, gained their powers through illegal (and racist) government experimentation. "What we wanted to do in the show is show that this is real," said Akil at the end of season 1. "Often black people are accused of being paranoid, but our paranoia is only paranoia until it becomes real, right? So the Flint water crisis, Tuskegee experiments, [the show's fictional drug] Green Light flooding the black communities with drugs and guns, we wanted to show that . . . and sort of explore it in a reality and not in a way most people would approach it."

The show's scope and world continues to expand in its third season—which, finally, includes Williams's Arrowverse debut. Getting him there wasn't easy.

"We worked very closely with the team at *Black Lightning* to make sure that it was more than a cameo, that it felt substantial," says crossover EP Marc Guggenheim. "It felt like we elevated the crossover to another level." Hopefully this is just beginning. ●

Unbroken
aR

ROW

HE'S FACED DEADSHOT, DAMIEN DARHK AND DEATHSTROKE. HOW WILL OLIVER QUEEN HANDLE HIS BIGGEST CHALLENGE YET: THE SERIES FINALE? BY CHANCELLOR AGARD • PHOTOGRAPHS BY CARLOS SERRAO

S

STEPHEN AMELL IS DREADING THE EIGHTH AND FINAL SEASON OF *Arrow,* though you wouldn't know it on this sunny July day in Los Angeles. Wearing Green Arrow's new suit, the CW star seems perfectly at ease as he strikes heroic pose after heroic pose on a dimly lit stage. But once he's traded heavy verdant leather for a T-shirt, jeans and baseball cap, his guard drops and the vulnerability starts to creep in as he contemplates *Arrow's* last 10 episodes, which begin production in three days. "I'm very emotional and melancholy, but it's time," Amell says as he takes a sip from a pint of Guinness. "I'm 38 years old, and I got this job when I was 30. I'd never had a job for more than a year. The fact that I've done this for the better part of a decade, and I'm not going to do it anymore, is a little frightening."

Developed by Greg Berlanti, Marc Guggenheim and Andrew Kreisberg, *Arrow* debuted in the fall of 2012. The DC Comics series follows billionaire playboy Oliver Queen (Amell), who, after years away, returned to now-Star City with one goal: to save his hometown as the hooded bow-and-arrow vigilante who

← Clockwise from left Oliver Queen (Stephen Amell) suited up for vigilante justice; the billionaire during his stay on the North China Sea island Lian Yu; tech genius Felicity Smoak (Emily Bett Rickards) goes glam; a Queen family portrait: Oliver's ex stepfather Walter Steele (Colin Salmon), left, mother Moira (Susanna Thompson) and sister Thea (Willa Holland) with Oliver.

Who's Who on Team Arrow

THROUGHOUT EIGHT SEASONS, SUPERHEROES HAVE COME AND GONE. HERE'S HOW ALL PAST AND PRESENT MEMBERS MADE THEIR MARK ON STAR CITY—PLUS SOME NOTABLE ENEMIES. *BY ALYSSA SMITH*

Oliver Queen

GREEN ARROW

STEPHEN AMELL

Presumed dead after five years lost at sea, the billionaire returned home and began an idealistic quest to save his city, armed with unlimited resources and a bow and arrow.

John Diggle

SPARTAN

DAVID RAMSEY

The former bodyguard and A.R.G.U.S. agent struggled with the dark side of vigilantism yet despite his reluctance, supported Team Arrow and earned his own hero alias.

Felicity Smoak

OVERWATCH

EMILY BETT RICKARDS

Computer expert Felicity joined Team Arrow in season 1—and eventually fell in love (and married) Oliver. In season 7's finale, she went into hiding to protect their daughter Mia.

Moira Queen

SUSANNA THOMPSON

The mother of Oliver and Thea, Moira was central to the season 1 conspiracy to destroy the Glades. After a confession and acquittal, she ran for mayor and was slain by Deathstroke.

Thea Queen
SPEEDY
WILLA HOLLAND
Oliver's sis fell under the spell of her real father, Malcolm Merlyn, after his identity was revealed. When his plots were dug up, she began a mission to undo his evil.

Roy Harper
ARSENAL
COLTON HAYNES
The ex-thief from the Glades dated Thea and fought bad guys as a member of Team Arrow, eventually leaving Star City with Thea to help her destroy the Lazarus Pits.

Tommy Merlyn
COLIN DONNELL
Oliver's childhood friend welcomed a changed Ollie back to their city but was quickly swept up in the Hood's murder spree. His death motivated Oliver to reconsider his dark path.

Malcolm Merlyn
DARK ARCHER
JOHN BARROWMAN
As a member of the League of Assassins, Malcolm originated multiple schemes against Oliver and Star City. In season 5, he sacrificed himself to save Thea.

Laurel Lance
BLACK CANARY/SIREN
KATIE CASSIDY RODGERS
An attorney for the city, Laurel began her vigilante work to continue her sister's legacy. After she was killed by Damien Darhk, Earth-2's Laurel assumed her place.

↑ Oliver trains with ally John Diggle (David Ramsey).

would become known as Green Arrow (it would take him four seasons to assume the moniker). What began as a solo crusade eventually grew to include former soldier John Diggle (David Ramsey), quirky computer genius Felicity Smoak (Emily Bett Rickards), lawyer-turned-hero Laurel Lance/Black Canary (Katie Cassidy Rodgers) and the rest of Team Arrow. Together they've defended their city from a host of threats—dark archers, megalomaniacal magicians—while flashbacks revealed what Oliver endured in the five years he was away, first shipwrecked and then honing his skills around the world to become *someone else, something else.*

The premiere gave the CW its most-watched series debut since 2009's *The Vampire Diaries.* But before they launched *Arrow,* Berlanti and Guggenheim had to suffer through a failure: 2011's *Green Lantern,* starring Ryan Reynolds. The duo were writers on the script but lost creative control of the film, which flopped. So when Warner Bros. Television president Peter Roth approached them in late 2011 about developing a *Green Arrow* show, they were wary. After much deliberation, Berlanti and Guggenheim agreed—on the condition that they maintain control. Says Guggenheim: "As long as we succeed or fail on our own work, then maybe this is worth a shot."

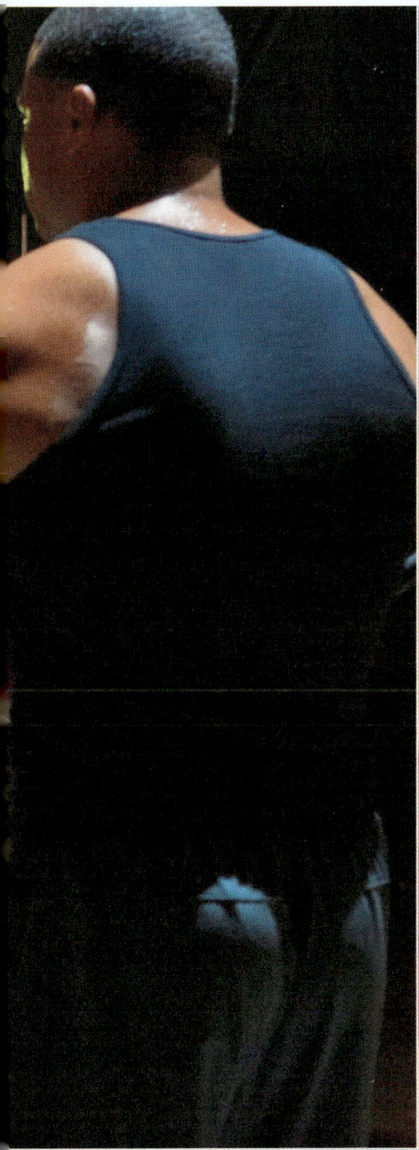

↑ Manu Bennett's Deathstroke in season 2.

← **Left to right** The Lance sisters, Sara (Caity Lotz) and Laurel (Katie Cassidy Rodgers), united; John and Felicity embrace.

↑ **From top** The villains: Malcolm Merlyn (John Barrowman); and Damien Darhk (Neal McDonough).

Their take on the Emerald Archer—who made his DC Comics debut in 1941—was noteworthy from the beginning. Taking cues from films like *The Bourne Identity* and series like *Homeland,* the writers imagined a dark, gritty and grounded show centered on a traumatized protagonist. "As we were breaking the story, we made very specific commitments to certain tonal things, such as 'At the end of act 1, he has his hands around his mother's throat.' And 'At the end of act 2, he kills a man in cold blood to protect his secret,'" says Guggenheim.

A hero committing murder? That was practically unheard of then. Having Oliver suit up in a veritable superhero costume by the pilot's climax was radical too. Sure, the Marvel Cinematic Universe was deep into phase 1 when the producers were developing *Arrow,* but TV was traditionally more apprehensive about comic books. *Smallville* famously had a "no tights, no flights" rule and only introduced superhero costumes in the last years of its 10-season run, and there weren't any masked avengers running around NBC's *Heroes* or ABC's *No Ordinary Family,* the latter produced by Berlanti. But *Arrow* not only fully committed to the idea of someone dressing up like Robin Hood to fight crime

Sara Lance
THE CANARY
CAITY LOTZ
A rescue by the League of Assassins after a shipwreck changed Sara's life forever, but her time on Team Arrow was cut short. After her resurrection she joined the Legends.

Quentin Lance
PAUL BLACKTHORNE
As police detective (later captain and then mayor), Quentin's secret alliance with Team Arrow helped keep his city safe even as it placed him in danger. He died saving Earth-2's Laurel.

Slade Wilson
DEATHSTROKE
MANU BENNETT
The masked merc started as Oliver's island mentor, then became a sworn enemy (who went on to murder mum Moira). Now they're cautious allies. It's complicated.

Curtis Holt
MISTER TERRIFIC
ECHO KELLUM
After discovering Oliver's secret identity, the Palmer Tech whiz and former Olympic medalist wanted in—and eventually suited up in his own gear to help Star City.

William Clayton
JACK MOORE/BEN LEWIS
Oliver was initially unaware of his son's existence because Moira Queen had paid the mom to disappear. It didn't help protect Will: He was kidnapped twice, and his mom was murdered.

Lyla Michaels
AUDREY MARIE ANDERSON
As the director of A.R.G.U.S., she's highly skeptical of Oliver's vigilantism. As Diggle's wife (twice—they had divorced), she's cautiously supportive of Team Arrow.

Damien Darhk
NEAL McDONOUGH
The ruthless leader of H.I.V.E., the magician Darhk spent more than a century plotting a world takeover before being slain by Oliver. (Don't worry, he's resurrected on *DC's Legends of Tomorrow*.)

Adrian Chase
PROMETHEUS
JOSH SEGARRA
The D.A. of Star City had a serial killer alter ego—and a grudge against Oliver. It all ended with Chase's dying after setting off a dead man's switch in an attempt to kill Thea and others.

Rene Ramirez
WILD DOG
RICK GONZALEZ
When Oliver recruited the Star City vigilante to join Team Arrow, he didn't expect Wild Dog to cut a deal with the FBI to testify against him. The two later made up.

Dinah Drake
BLACK CANARY
JULIANA HARKAVY
Unlike her Canary predecessor Laurel, that sonic cry was all natural: Dinah is a meta-human. When her vocal cords got damaged, she continued to fight at Arrow's side.

↑ Diggle as the Spartan, Oliver, and sis Thea as Speedy.

with a bow and arrow, it introduced a second costumed rogue, the Huntress (Jessica De Gouw), in episode 7. Yet restraint was essential when it came to Oliver's cowl. "It's really easy to make a guy with a bow and arrow look silly. We sweated every detail," Guggenheim says of getting four-time Oscar winner Colleen Atwood (*Memoirs of a Geisha*) to design the suit. "We had so many conversations to get it approved," adds Berlanti. "We were determined to show we could do on TV what they were doing in the movies every six months."

Beyond "grounded and real," there wasn't much of a plan in the early years, which allowed the show to naturally evolve—from introducing more DC characters, such as Deathstroke (Manu Bennett) and Roy Harper (Colton Haynes), sooner than they initially intended, to promoting Emily Bett Rickards's Felicity from a one-off character in the show's third episode to a series regular in season 2 and eventually Oliver's wife. Even the whole idea of a Team Arrow—which, over time, added Rene Ramirez/Wild Dog (Rick Gonzalez) and Dinah Drake/Black Canary (Juliana Harkavy)—was the result of the writers allowing the best ideas to guide the story. "Greg used to say all the time, 'You have a hit TV show until you don't, so don't save s---,'" says Amell.

Also not planned: *Arrow* spawning an entire shared universe. "We

went on record a lot of times during the premiere of the pilot saying, 'No superpowers, no time travel.' But midway through season 1, Greg started to harbor a notion of doing the Flash," says Guggenheim. "When it comes to creating a universe, the pitfall is that people try to run before they can walk. The key is, you build it show by show." And so they did. First, they introduced *The Flash* star Grant Gustin's Barry Allen in the two-part mid-season finale of *Arrow*'s second season. From there, *Supergirl* took flight in 2015, then *DC's Legends of Tomorrow* in 2016, and *Batwoman* this fall. But even though *Arrow* is the universe's namesake, Amell doesn't concern himself with the sibling series outside of the now-annual crossovers. "I want all of them to do great, but they're not my responsibility," he says. "My responsibility is *Arrow*, and to make sure everyone from the cast to the crew are good."

That said, the universe's expansion precipitated what is widely considered to be *Arrow*'s best season, the fifth one. After focusing on magic in season 4, the show returned to its street-crime roots as part of "a concerted effort to play not just to our strengths but what made the shows unique," Guggenheim says of balancing their four superseries at the time. "Because *Arrow* was the longest-running Arrowverse show, we were able to do something that none of the other shows could do, which is have a villain who was basically born out of the events of season 1," he explains of introducing Adrian Chase/Prometheus (Josh Segarra), whose criminal father was killed by Oliver. "That gave the season a resonance."

↑ **From top** Tech whiz Curtis Holt (Echo Kellum) helps Felicity (alongside Rick Gonzalez as Rene Ramirez) in the lab; Oliver, Felicity and son Will Clayton (Jack Moore).

It was midway through season 6 when Amell realized he was ready to hang up Oliver Queen's hood. "It was just time to move on," he says of pitching that Oliver leave the series at the end of season 7. Berlanti persuaded him to return for one final season, which the producers decided would be the end. "We all felt in our gut it was the right time," says Berlanti. Adds Berlanti Productions president Sarah Schechter: "It's such a

↑ From top Oliver's half sister Emiko Queen (Sea Shimooka) with her minions; Felicity visits Oliver in prison.

Emiko Queen
GREEN ARROW
SEA SHIMOOKA
Oliver's half sister picked up his mantle in season 7, but it was to destroy Oliver's legacy. She ultimately repents—but too late: She died at the hands of her former allies.

Ricardo Diaz
DRAGON
KIRK ACEVEDO
When the underworld kingpin found his illegal empire destroyed by Oliver, he swore revenge. Eventually it didn't go well for him—he was slain by Emiko.

Connor Hawke
GREEN ARROW
JOSEPH DAVID-JONES
In the year 2040 the adopted son of Diggle and Lyla helps keep Star City safe as an agent of Knightwatch. It's the second version of this character shown in the 'verse.

Mia Smoak
BLACKSTAR
KATHERINE McNAMARA
The daughter of Oliver and Felicity, Mia is born in 2019. In 2040 she works by the side of Dinah, Roy and others to protect Star City against the Galaxy One company.

John Diggle Jr.
CHARLIE BARNETT
In 2040 the son of Diggle and Lyla has gone down a dark path: He leads an underworld gang. (Trivia point: J.J. didn't exist in the erased Flashpoint timeline; Diggle had a daughter instead.)

privilege to be able to say when something's ending as opposed to having something just ripped away."

But there's one integral cast member who won't be around to see *Arrow* through its final season: Rickards filmed her final episode in 2019. Continuing the show without Team Arrow's heart is "not great," says Amell. But "*Arrow,* as you know it, has effectively ended," he adds. "It's a different show in season 8." And he's not exaggerating.

The final season finds Oliver working for the all-seeing extraterrestrial the Monitor (LaMonica Garrett) and trying to save the multiverse from a cataclysmic event. "[We're] taking the show on the road, really getting away from Star City," says Guggenheim. "Oliver is going to be traveling the world." Adds showrunner Beth Schwartz: "This is sort of his final test because it's greater than Star City." Along the way he will head down memory lane, with actor Colin Donnell, who played Oliver's best friend, Tommy Merlyn, in season 1, and Segarra's Adrian Chase making appearances. "Episode 1 is an ode to season 1, and episode 2 is an ode to season 3," explains Amell. "We're playing our greatest hits." If only we could request an encore. ●

HITS & MISSES

The Bullseye

WE'RE PRETTY SURE STAR CITY HIGH HAS AN ARCHERY CLUB

A bit far-fletched

A killer Queen

Aiming to be the very best

Team Daddy issues

Give this sidekick a promotion!

You don't know the power of Darhk's side

Ra's all here

Stephen Amell

AFTER EIGHT SEASONS, ARROW PREPARES FOR THE END. THE ACTOR REFLECTS ON HIS ORIGIN STORY AND SAYS GOODBYE TO THE SUPERHERO THAT MADE HIM A STAR. BY CHANCELLOR AGARD

Q+A

TEN EPISODES. THAT'S ALL THAT STANDS BETWEEN ACTOR STEPHEN Amell and the conclusion of his long-running CW series *Arrow* when *EW* spoke to him. "I'm legitimately frightened about the end of it," says Amell. Yet looking back, the 38-year-old realizes just how lucky he was to score the game-changing role. "If they had said to me, 'You need to pay us $2,500 per episode to be Oliver Queen in season 1.' I would have said yes. It was the opportunity of a lifetime." With his time in the cowl coming to a close, Amell reminisces about his audition all those years ago and explains what it was like reading those final scripts.

From talking to the *Arrow* producers, I know you were the first person to audition for this role. What do you remember about that experience?

STEPHEN AMELL So I went to a hockey game with my cousin Robbie [Amell] on a Saturday night, and he goes, "Have you gotten an audition for *Arrow* yet?" And I go, "No, what's *Arrow*?" He goes,

PHOTOGRAPH BY MATTHIAS CLAMER

"It's based on the Green Arrow." He goes, "Well, I read the pilot, and I pictured you the entire time that I was reading it." He's like, "I've got an audition, but I actually don't want to go, because you are going to get cast in this role." I went in [to audition], and David Nutter was there, Marc Guggenheim, Andrew Kreisberg. Greg [Berlanti] was in his office, because he was like, "If you find someone interesting, let me know." And I went in, read, and Dave Nutter looked at me, and he goes, "Can you go outside for a couple minutes?" And I go, "Yeah, for sure." And I came back into the room, and there are 11 more people there, and they just had me read again.... I got the job the following Tuesday morning.

What was it like adjusting to the physical demands of the role?
I loved it. I loved all of it. Doing a lot of the stuff that I did in the pilot was proof of concept for the series. I had to do it. In episode 2, episode 3, episode 4, I had to do it, period, because photographically when you do stunts, they were able to film me doing it. They were able to shoot on my face, and if we didn't continue on in that manner, something would have been missing.

When did you realize the show was becoming a hit? Was it during that first season?
People think that the height of the show is when it's premiering, when my torso is 90 ft. tall on Sunset Boulevard. That's not it. It actually compounds over the years, and people become really, really big fans because of the amount of content that you're pushing up, right? I didn't realize that the show was a giant hit until 2017, when I was on an island called Panarea, which was off the coast of Lipari, which is off the coast of Sicily. It's so small, there aren't even cars—golf carts, that's it. We walked into this restaurant that looked closed, and this woman walks out. We're like, "Are you guys open?" And she goes, "Si, Arrow." I'm like, "Are you f---ing kidding me?"

"I JUST HOPE THAT WE GET TO DO ALL THE THINGS THAT WE WANT TO DO"

—STEPHEN AMELL, ON THE FINAL SEASON OF *ARROW*

→ **Clockwise from left** Juliana Harkavy, Emily Bett Rickards, Echo Kellum, David Ramsey, Rick Gonzalez, Stephen Amell and Colton Haynes.

↓ Amell in season 1 as the Hood.

Fast-forward to now: What did it feel like when you started getting the scripts for *Arrow*'s final season?
It was weird, actually, because [executive producer] Beth [Schwartz] just had her first kiddo, and so the writers room, instead of taking a break after the season ended, worked through. Her assistant sent me episode 801 two weeks after we wrapped. I didn't read it for four weeks because I needed some time to reset. I'm so excited about them. I just hope that we get to do all the things that we want to do. Don't leave anything in the quiver.

PHOTOGRAPH BY BEN WATTS

Struck by Cupid's Arrow

The Emerald Archer usually ends up with the Black Canary. That was before fans saw red-hot sparks flying between **FELICITY SMOAK** and **OLIVER QUEEN**. BY RICH SANDS

WHEN IT COMES TO TAKING A BREAK from a relationship, Ross and Rachel have nothing on Oliver and Felicity. As *Arrow* flies through its final season, Oliver (Stephen Amell) is off saving the multiverse from a crisis across infinite earths—and purportedly slated to die in the process—while his wife, Felicity (Emily Bett Rickards), will have to wait until 2040 to reconnect with her long-lost love. For passionate fans of the so-called "Olicity" pairing, the wait will be a crisis of its own—and may not be fully satisfying, since Rickards has left the

↑ **Clockwise from left** Oliver and Felicity in season 6; the couple share an intimate dinner; together with Oliver's son (and Felicity's stepson) Will Clayton (Jack Moore)

> **YOU ARE MY ALWAYS, AND I JUST WANT THE CHANCE TO BE YOURS"**
>
> —OLIVER QUEEN

show, and the final few episodes of *Arrow* will be swept up in "Crisis."

That's high stakes for a relationship that was never part of the show's original plan. Felicity (a minor character in the DC Comics lore) was originally slated for just one episode as a Queen Consolidated IT staffer who helped Oliver with a computer issue. But when producers noticed the sparkling onscreen chemistry between Amell and Rickards, they folded the character into the story line, with Felicity joining Team Arrow as a tech expert. Though Oliver feared he wasn't suited for romance, his relentless brooding was ultimately no match for her adorable quirkiness, and by the end of the third season they were finally in a full-fledged relationship.

Not that it's been happily ever after in Star City. First, diehard comic-book fans had to accept that *Arrow* was not beholden to the DC canon, where Green Arrow and Black Canary are frequently linked. More important, Oliver and Felicity's relationship has been tested by the life-or-death stakes of superhero life. And let's not forget that Oliver, who has struggled with the trauma and darkness resulting from his five-year odyssey after being shipwrecked, is not exactly the poster child for honesty and emotional vulnerability.

Their first engagement (in season 4) ended after Felicity found out that Oliver had a secret son. (Oops!) Still, they went through with a fake wedding as part of a plan to draw out a villain, and Oliver stuck with his planned vows. "With your kindness, your generosity, your compassion, your intelligence, your wit and your trust, you brought me into the light," he told her. "You let me know that I deserved it. You were that light. And I don't know if I still deserve that trust, if I deserve you. I probably don't. But whatever has happened, whatever will happen, the way that you make me feel is the best part of my life.... You are my always, and I just want the chance to be yours."

Later, when they got married for real during season 6—hijacking the wedding of Barry Allen and Iris West at the tail end of the "Crisis on Earth-X" crossover—Felicity offered a foreboding oath. "I believe that no matter what life throws at us, our love can conquer it," she said. "My greatest fear in life is losing you." The one arrow Oliver couldn't avoid, it turns out, was Cupid's. ●

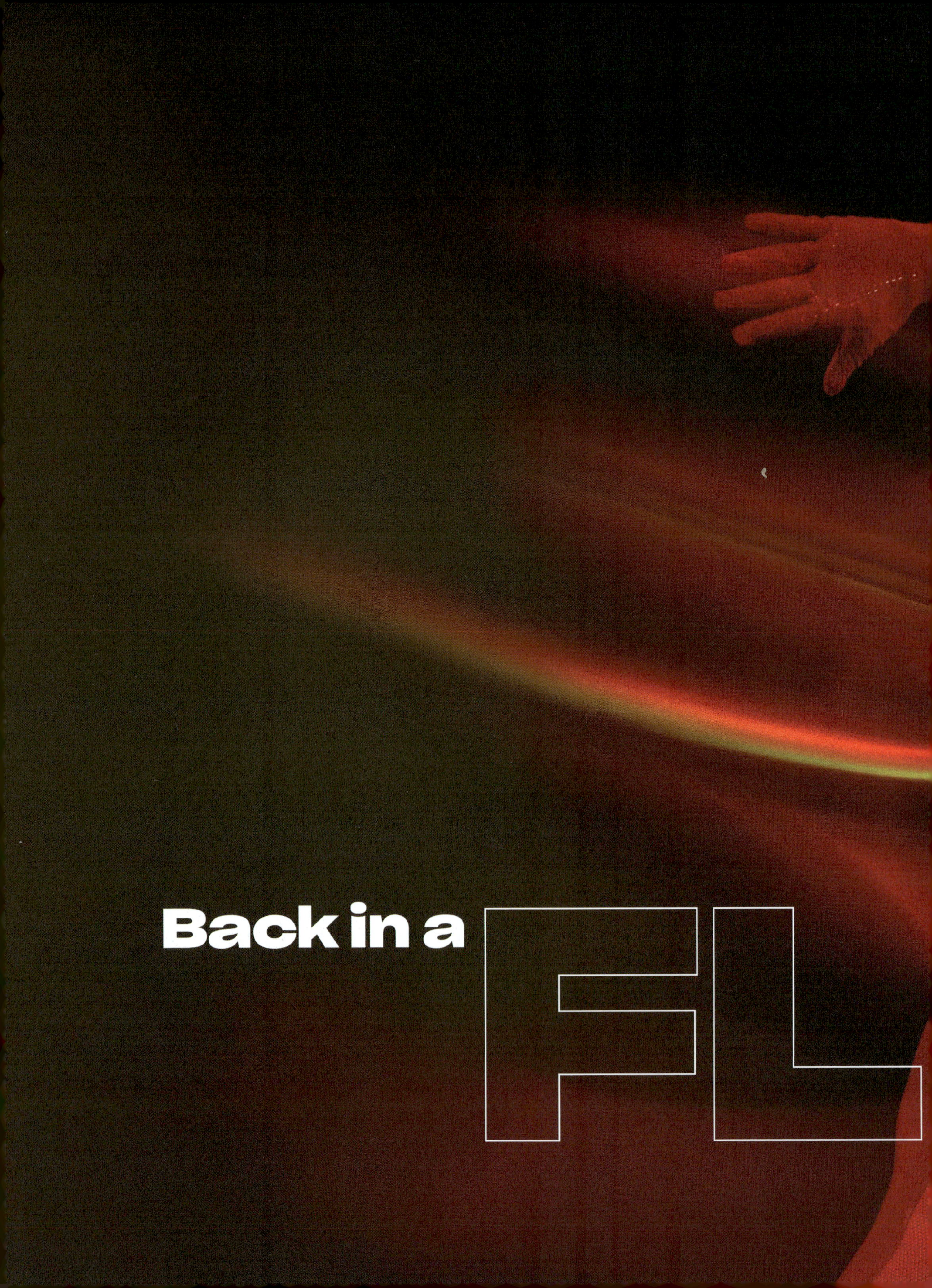

Back in a FL

ash

IT WAS THE FIRST SHOW TO SPIN OFF—AND QUICKLY WON A PLACE IN FANBOYS' HEARTS. HERE'S WHAT'S NEXT FOR BARRY ALLEN AND TEAM FLASH. BY RICH SANDS • PHOTOGRAPHS BY CARLOS SERRAO

W

WHEN KINDHEARTED 11-YEAR-OLD Barry Allen couldn't outrun a group of middle school bullies, his mother offered comfort by telling him, "It's better to have a good heart than fast legs."

The producers of *The Flash* wondered: "Why not both?" To that end, the first 'verse spinoff has always sought to combine dazzling sci-fi adventures with poignant, character-driven storytelling. And that's exactly why executive producer Greg Berlanti wanted to make the show in the first place. "*The Flash* was the one I was the most emotionally invested in [as a child]," Berlanti told *EW* in 2014. "At the end of the day, you never thought he would be the one to save everybody, but he was."

Barry Allen, a forensic scientist who was hit by lightning and doused by chemicals to become the fastest man alive, made his DC Comics book debut in 1956. A founding member of the Justice League of America, the character became hugely popular. CBS even gave the Scarlet Speedster his first prime-time showcase in 1990-91, starring John Wesley Shipp.

For their version of Barry, Berlanti & Co. knew they needed to find an actor who could handle the optimistic spirit they wanted for the spinoff. "We were looking for someone who was relatable, someone that was an everyman who was bestowed with superpowers—someone a little bit goofy," casting director David Rapaport says.

Rapaport immediately zeroed in on Grant Gustin, who was coming off a breakout supporting role on *Glee* as Sebastian Smythe, the charmingly conniving lead singer of the Dalton Academy Warblers. Despite not sporting the traditional blond hair of his comic-book counterpart, Gustin was otherwise ideal for Barry's optimistic persona. "I just tried to be a real guy and leave it at that," he told *EW* in 2014 of his audition. "Let all the superhero stuff come later."

Gustin made his debut in a well-received *Arrow* two-parter in December 2013, and the CW quickly gave the green light for a *Flash* pilot. Producers established "heart, humor and spectacle" as

← **Clockwise from left** Barry Allen (Grant Gustin) in season 1, pictured with then-Iris West (Candice Patton), Det. Eddie Thawne (Rick Cosnett) and Joe West (Jesse L. Martin); Earth 1's Harrison Wells (Tom Cavanaugh) was actually the Reverse-Flash, who had murdered him and taken his identity; Team Flash pals Cisco Ramon (Carlos Valdes) and Caitlin Snow (Danielle Panabaker).

Who's Who on Team Flash

S.T.A.R. LABS' EXPLOSION CREATED A WHOLE LOT OF META-HUMANS. HERE'S WHO CLEANED UP THE MESS—AND WHO JOINED TEAM FLASH TO PROTECT CENTRAL CITY FROM FUTURE DISASTERS. *BY ALYSSA SMITH*

Barry Allen

THE FLASH

GRANT GUSTIN

When the fastest man alive's not messing up the timeline (hello, Flashpoint), he's saving the world. But some things will never change; the Scarlet Speedster has always been in love with Iris.

Iris West-Allen

CANDICE PATTON

The unacknowledged leader of Team Flash is Barry's biggest supporter and oldest childhood friend. Iris, an intrepid journalist with a strong sense of justice, recently founded *The Central City Citizen* newspaper.

Joe West

JESSE L. MARTIN

After Barry's mother was murdered and his father was falsely jailed for it, Joe took in and raised Barry as his own. He's also the current police captain and father figure to Team Flash.

Wally West

KID FLASH

KEIYNAN LONSDALE

He wasn't raised by Joe West (when Joe's marriage ended, mom Francine disappeared while pregnant), but he's part of the family now—and a fellow meta-human speedster.

Harrison Wells
TOM CAVANAGH

Earth-1's Wells was murdered by the Reverse-Flash long before season 1, but there's a whole universe of Wellses out there who joined Team Flash, including Earth-19's H.R. Wells and Earth-221's Sherloque.

Caitlin Snow
KILLER FROST

DANIELLE PANABAKER

After Flashpoint, the S.T.A.R. Labs scientist began to exhibit superpowers that came with a dark side: an evil alternate personality.

Cisco Ramon
VIBE

CARLOS VALDES

The engineering genius developed the ability to manipulate energy after being exposed to dark matter, but once he created a cure, he elected to return to being "just" human.

Eddie Thawne
RICK COSNETT

Iris's fiancé and ancestor to the Reverse-Flash (Eobard Thawne) sacrificed himself to erase Eobard from existence.

Jay Garrick
THE FLASH

JOHN WESLEY SHIPP

Earth-3's semi-retired version of the Flash has joined Barry on many missions, including fighting against Savitar and Zoom.

Ralph Dibny
ELONGATED MAN

HARTLEY SAWYER

The ex-police detective was hit by dark matter and now is Barry's super-stretchy sidekick and fellow vigilante.

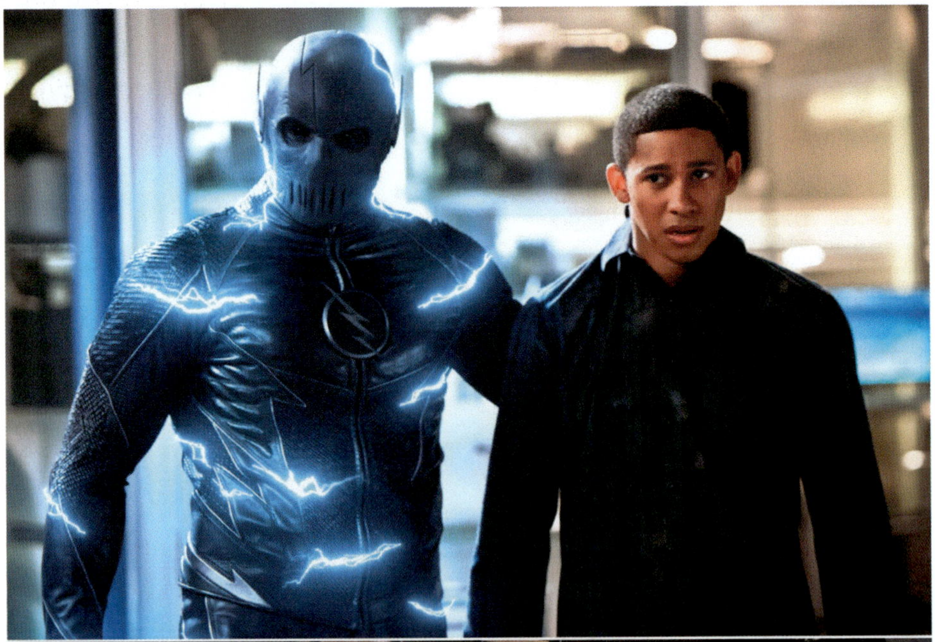

↑ **From top** Wally West (Keiynan Lonsdale) being kidnapped by the villain Zoom; Barry interrogates the Reverse-Flash (Matt Letscher).

their guiding formula, an homage to the comic-book origins as well as a complement to *Arrow*'s darker tone. Though Barry was haunted by the mysterious murder of his mother years before and his father's subsequent conviction for the crime, he never lost his positivity. His belief in his dad's innocence ultimately led him to become a crime-scene investigator.

The pilot introduced a strong supporting ensemble, including Barry's surrogate father, Det. Joe West (Jesse L. Martin), and his daughter Iris (Candice Patton), the object of Barry's unrequited crush. S.T.A.R. Laboratories scientists Harrison Wells (Tom Cavanagh, in one of many roles he's played over the run of the series), Cisco Ramon (Carlos Valdes) and Caitlin Snow (Danielle Panabaker) helped Barry master his superspeed and take on freakishly powered meta-human criminals.

The show bowed in October 2014 and was an immediate hit, scoring the CW's second-largest premiere audience ever. And that was no Flash in the pan: The series has remained the network's top-rated show for five seasons running.

↑ **From top** XS (Jessica Parker Kennedy); the Flash comforts Iris.

Though flashy (pun intended) comic-book adventures provide the "spectacle" portion of the producers' mantra (see: over-the-top villains like Gorilla Grodd and King Shark), the series has always striven to remain grounded in the personal relationships of its core characters. "These are people who are 3-D, fully fleshed out," says executive producer Eric Wallace, who took over as showrunner for season 6. "People we could recognize in our real life if it wasn't for their powers. Joe West is the dad we all want. Cisco is the best friend I wish I had my whole life. Iris is the partner that anyone would be lucky to have. So when you see these people coming into your house every week, it is like family."

One key factor in the show's popularity has been the relationship between Barry and Iris. By the end of the second season, he had finally won her over, to the delight of #WestAllen shippers across the Internet. They wed during season 4 and have had a surprisingly resilient romance for a prime-time TV couple, especially one that has been exposed to supervillains (who could forget Iris's fearless dive off a building to save her shackled husband from Rag Doll?), alternate realities and the unexpected arrival of their fully grown daughter from the future.

That daughter, Nora West-Allen (Jessica Parker Kennedy), met a heartbreaking demise at the end of last season, erased from existence after her well-intentioned but poorly executed plan to save her father altered the timeline. It also set the stage for this season's "Crisis on Infinite Earths" crossover. In a callout to a key moment in comic-book lore that had been seeded way back in the first episode, a future edition of *The Central City Citizen* with the ominous headline "Flash Missing Vanishes in Crisis" now features a 2019 dateline, five years earlier than originally shown.

"When we showed the newspaper article, I was like, so we have to go 10 years or that's a big gamble," Gustin remembers of that momentous Easter egg. "We've found a smart way to kind of get there a little sooner, and we're going to get to see a payoff. And I think we've earned it. That's what's so good about these crossovers every year. Everything that we do in them is so emotional and so exciting because we earn it throughout our seasons."

And while the crossover is sure to be a pivotal point for the season, what Gustin appreciates most about the show is how they will find a way to balance that with emotion. "What I will always love the most about this job is when we get to kind of stop and do real scene work and get to look each other in the eye and say what we're thinking, what we're feeling," he says. "It's always what's made our show stand out, the heart that we all try to put into it." That's something sure to keep the Flash running into the future. ●

ADDITIONAL REPORTING > CHANCELLOR AGARD, SAMANTHA HIGHFILL AND BREIA BRISSEY

← **From top** XS, the Flash and Vibe (Cisco's hero alter ego) discuss terms with King Shark; a family Thanksgiving.

Jesse Wells

JESSE QUICK

VIOLETT BEANE

The speedster daughter of Earth-2's Harrison Wells, Jesse falls for Wally when she's on Earth-1 but ultimately leaves to lead her own team.

Clifford DeVoe

THE THINKER

NEIL SANDILANDS

The criminal mastermind who orchestrated the bus dark-matter accident that created many new meta-humans met his end at the hands of his ex-wife.

Cecile Horton

DANIELLE NICOLET

She's the D.A. of Central City, the girlfriend of Joe West, the mother of his daughter Jenna, and also a meta-human telepath ally of Team Flash.

Nora West-Allen

XS

JESSICA PARKER KENNEDY

The time-traveling, misled speedster daughter of Barry and Iris, she's erased from existence after young Cicada is given the meta-human cure.

Orlin Dwyer and Grace Gibbons

CICADA

CHRIS KLEIN AND SARAH CARTER

This meta-human team keeps serial killing in the family. Thankfully Team Flash defeats both.

Hunter Zolomon

ZOOM

TEDDY SEARS

A speedster serial killer from Earth-2, he's responsible for Henry Allen's murder. Today he's presumed dead.

Grant Gustin

COMING OFF A HEART-BREAKING SEASON 5 FINALE OF THE FLASH, THE ACTOR REFLECTS ON THAT DIFFICULT NORA STORY LINE—AND FLASHES FORWARD TO HIS END-GAME HOPES AND DREAMS.

BY CHANCELLOR AGARD

Q+A

GRANT GUSTIN MAY HAVE MADE HIS DEBUT AS BARRY Allen on *Arrow,* but in the blink of an eye the 29-year-old actor and his series *The Flash* carved their own unique, thrilling place in the superhero pantheon. Five seasons later Gustin still considers himself the consummate fanboy (awww!). He takes *EW* back to those early days as the speedster—and makes the case for Kid Flash.

You made your debut in this world on the second season of *Arrow.* Can you take us back to what was going through your head when you filmed that episode?

GRANT GUSTIN I was really nervous. Obviously I just binge-watched all of *Arrow,* which I don't recommend doing. If you've seen it, great, but don't binge it all right before you go work on it, because I was starstruck by everybody, like shook. I couldn't act normally around anyone. So that was kind of going through my head, that I had just watched the whole first season. The first scene I shot was, I think, the first time we see me—it was Barry getting off the train in the rain in Star City and going to the crime scene, and I had my case with me. It was just surreal, man. I was just kind of thrown right into it.

Has that sort of fanboy feeling disappeared in the past five years or so?

No. It kind of comes in waves though. Day in and day out of *Flash* is, it's definitely become a job and it's a grind, and I work long days,

PHOTOGRAPH BY BEN WATTS

as do most of the cast and all of the crew. But there's always something, like last year when we did the crossovers and Tyler Hoechlin was working as Superman a lot, and I got to be on-set with Superman for the first time. That was a big moment for me. And then being in the Fortress of Solitude was a mind-blowing moment. I get to be the Flash on TV surrounded by all these other superheroes, and it's something I don't ever want to take for granted.

"I WAS STARSTRUCK BY EVERYBODY, LIKE SHOOK. I COULDN'T ACT NORMALLY AROUND ANYONE"

—GRANT GUSTIN ON HIS *ARROW* DEBUT

As you look back on season 5 of *The Flash*, what was the most interesting aspect for you?
The Nora aspect is probably the thing that was my whole season, really. And it was tough. It's weird introducing a daughter [played by Jessica Parker Kennedy] who's more or less our age and to play the dynamic of "That's my daughter." To be a father suddenly, but you have no history really with this person. It was an interesting dynamic to play, and it evolved in a way that was so heartbreaking. I didn't know that it was going to go where it went throughout the season with just the struggle that existed between Nora, Barry and Iris, and then just the devastating way that we kind of wrapped it up. It was just a tough arc to do.

What are your hopes for the future of *The Flash* and for the universe in general?
I don't really know, to be honest. I've learned to not have too many expectations for a season or for an episode because it almost never goes where I think it's going to go. [There are] little things I want to explore. We have to see the Reverse-Flash villain [again]. He's the big bad of the series, as far as I'm concerned. So we have to see that tied up. I want to see Kid Flash [Keiynan Lonsdale] come back and do some cool stuff. Jay Garrick [John Wesley Shipp]—I think we need to tie up that story line too. Those are the three characters that kind of pop in my head that I'd like to see more of in the coming seasons and wrap up their story lines before we wrap up our series.

→ **Opposite, clockwise from left** Candice Patton, Tom Cavanagh, Jessica Parker Kennedy, Danielle Panabaker, Carlos Valdes, Danielle Nicolet, Grant Gustin and Hartley Sawyer.

↓ Left: Barry's first appearance with Oliver Queen. Right: the West-Allen family.

Jesse Wells
EARTH-2
The daughter of Wells developed superspeed (and a cool new nickname with it, Jesse Quick!). At first she was beating a few of Barry's early records, but where she lagged behind was in stamina, such as during "Enter Flashtime," when she dropped out.

Barry Allen
EARTH-1
In season 1 it was a big deal for Barry to hit Mach 2 for a split second—now that number is laughable. Leaving the speedforce and time-travel out of it, at one point he outran a lightning bolt (200,000 mph).

Hunter Zolomon
EARTH-2
The serial-killing speedster Zoom wasn't fast enough to create a speed mirage, a task Barry accomplished easily, and even after stealing some of Barry's powers, he couldn't keep up in a one-on-one race—not that it matters anymore.

Barry 'Savitar' Allen
EARTH-1
Without his suit this Barry time remnant was exactly as fast as the original Barry was during the Flashpoint incident. When he was wearing his metallic armor—which emits a white lightning and deflects bullets—he was even faster.

Who's Really the

His name is **BARRY ALLEN,** and he's constantly in a race to prove he's the fastest man alive. (Spoiler

ILLUSTRATIONS BY MARTIN GEE

Wally West
EARTH-1
Iris's younger brother first faced off against Flash in season 3, a race Barry handily won. Since then, he trained up, and in a race against Jessie and Barry, he beat the track time by 0.21 seconds, which was fast enough to stop Savitar in the third-season finale.

Nora Allen-West
EARTH-1
The future daughter of Barry and Iris would, of course, be pretty darn quick. Not only was she fast enough to make the trip back in time, but she could access the Negative Speed Force, which harnesses bad emotions and creates a tachyon supercharge.

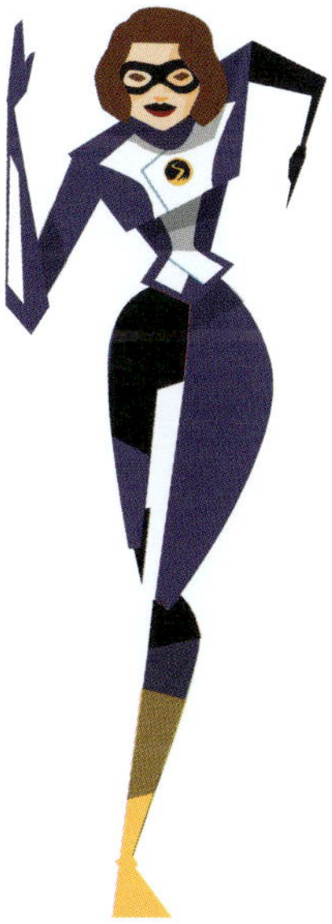

Eobard Thawne
EARTH-1
There were at least two different Reverse-Flashes: one created by Barry's Flashpoint, and a much faster and more experienced version of himself, who spent decades perfecting his speed-capturing device as the scientist Harry Wells.

Jay Garrick
EARTH-3
When Barry first met the Crimson Comet, he had suffered for years under the influence of Zoom's speed-dampening device. While he seemed to recover, after a recent incident betrayed his slowing stamina, he announced his retirement.

Fastest?

He is!) We investigate the records of his fellow speedsters. BY ALYSSA SMITH

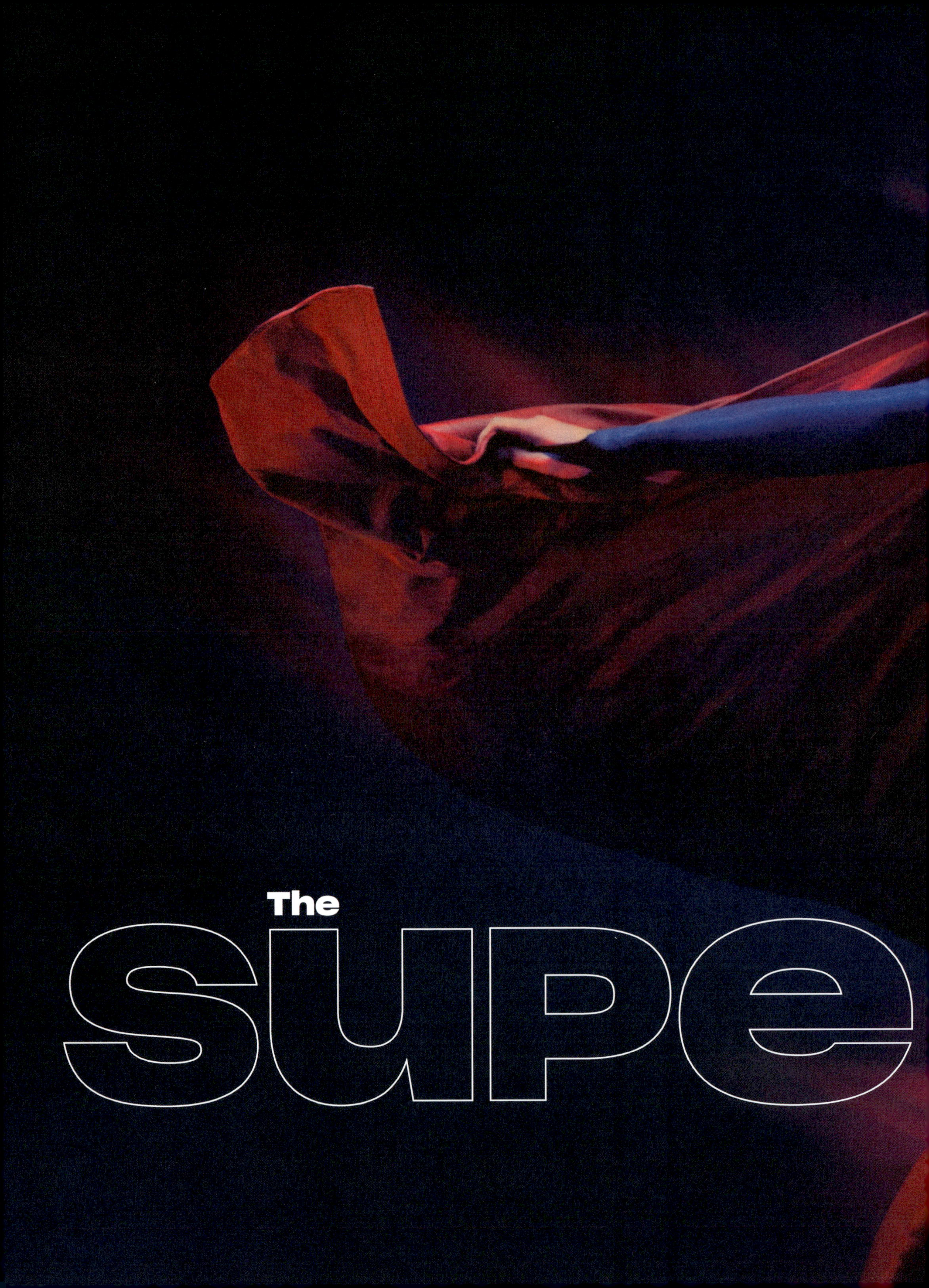

The Supe

RGiRL

Next Door

SHE MOVED FROM CBS TO THE CW, AND NOW THE REPORTER-SUPERHERO EVOLVES ONCE AGAIN FOR THE SERIES' FIFTH SEASON.

BY GINA McINTYRE AND CHANCELLOR AGARD • PHOTOGRAPHS BY CARLOS SERRAO

IT'S NOT EASY BEING SUPER—THE outsize expectations, the requisite spandex, the overwhelming sense of duty. But from the start actress Melissa Benoist and her onscreen alter ego Kara Zor-El were more than up to the task. Now that the actress has soared into the fifth season of the CW's *Supergirl,* which debuted Oct. 6, she's proud of her heroine's journey. "Kara is always evolving and becoming more of a woman," explains the actress. But while "it's so fun to look back on season 1 and see how much she has grown," Benoist admits it wasn't until season 4 that she connected deeply with the Girl of Steel: "I just felt an ownership and responsibility, and [I knew] what I wanted [the role] to mean to other people."

In the four years since the comic-book adventure premiered with an enviable time slot on CBS and sky-high expectations, Kara has come to mean quite a lot to the nearly 13 million people who tuned in Oct. 26, 2015. Like her famous cousin Kal-El, Kara escaped the doomed planet of Krypton just before its destruction. Then 13 years old, Kara was supposed to follow the infant Superman to Earth to watch over him, but her spaceship was knocked off course, landing in an interstellar time warp, where she was stuck for 24 years. When she finally arrived at her destination, Kal-El had been flying around saving the day for years, and Kara was still just a teen.

← Clockwise from left Director of the Department of Extra-Normal Operations Hank Henshaw, later revealed to be the alien J'onn J'onzz (David Harewood), with Kara Zor-El (Melissa Benoist) and Agent Alex Danvers (Chyler Leigh); Superman (Tyler Hoechlin) and cousin Supergirl; while in her civilian garb, Kara uses the name of her adopted family, Danvers, pictured here with editor boss Cat Grant (Calista Flockhart).

Who's Who on Earth-38

SUPERGIRL'S EARTH IS FULL OF ALIEN REFUGEES FROM PLANETS LIKE KRYPTON, MARS AND DAXAM. NATIONAL CITY'S HUMANS HAVEN'T KEPT OPINIONS OF THEIR NEW NEIGHBORS TO THEMSELVES. *BY ALYSSA SMITH*

Kara Zor-El

KARA DANVERS/ SUPERGIRL

MELISSA BENOIST

Raised in the Danvers family after arriving on Earth, Kara's bond with sis Alex is her guiding light—as strong as her sense of justice and desire to help as many people, human or otherwise, as she can.

Alex Danvers

CHYLER LEIGH

When Kara was first adopted into Alex's family, the budding genius felt overshadowed, but soon the two became true sisters. Today the bioengineer and doctor serves as the D.E.O.'s director.

J'onn J'onzz

HANK HENSHAW/ JOHN JONES/ MARTIAN MAN HUNTER

DAVID HAREWOOD

The green martian adopted the form of Hank after meeting the agent in order to reform the D.E.O.; eventually forced to resign, he's now a private detective.

James Olsen

GUARDIAN

MEHCAD BROOKS

Clark Kent sends his trusted friend to watch over his cousin, and Olsen does so by joining CatCo. Later, when he becomes the crime fighter Guardian, he's ironically unmasked.

Winn Schott
MAN IN THE VAN
JEREMY JORDAN
Kara's closest friend at CatCo also designed her costume. Because of his tech smarts, he's recruited by Brainy to join him in the 31st century.

Cat Grant
CALISTA FLOCKHART
The founder of CatCo (and Kara's boss) saw Supergirl as her paper's ticket to fame; later she becomes the White House's press secretary.

Maggie Sawyer
FLORIANA LIMA
The Science Police detective (and ex-fiancée of Alex) runs support for Supergirl through official channels.

Mon-El
MIKE MATTHEWS
CHRIS WOOD
The former prince of the destroyed planet Daxam began dating Kara after arriving on Earth; later he's forced into the 31st century, where he founds a Legion of Super-Heroes.

Lena Luthor
KATIE McGRATH
Being the half sister of Lex doesn't make her bad. The brilliant CEO first allies with Supergirl, but it turns sour when Kara's deceptions are revealed.

Samantha Arias
REIGN
ODETTE ANNABLE
Before her Kryptonian abilities began to manifest and take over her human personality, the single mom was a good friend to Kara and Lena.

↑ From top Rhea, queen of the planet Daxam (Teri Hatcher), looks on as her son Mon-El (Chris Wood) says goodbye; the Danvers parents, Eliza (Helen Slater) and Jeremiah (Dean Cain).

Believing that Kara would benefit from the same type of normal upbringing he had enjoyed, Superman placed her in the care of a scientist couple who helped him understand his powers, the Danverses—who, in a brilliant bit of casting, are played by Dean Cain, who appeared as the Big Blue Boy Scout on *Lois & Clark,* and Helen Slater, who starred in the 1984 film *Supergirl.* Their teenage daughter Alex became Kara's adoptive sister.

Years later, as a young woman in National City, Kara tried to conceal her powers, working as an assistant to National City media mogul Cat Grant (Calista Flockhart). But after a plane ferrying Alex (Chyler Leigh) to Europe for a conference nearly crashed and Kara flew to her rescue, she decided to pursue the hero life after all—with some assistance from recent Metropolis transplant James Olsen (Mehcad Brooks) and office buddy Winn Schott (Jeremy Jordan). Soon Kara learned that Alex had a secret of her own—she was a top officer with the D.E.O., a covert agency created to protect Earth from the threat of alien invasion—and the sisters got to work saving the world.

When translating a character introduced in 1959 for today's audiences, *Supergirl* creators Greg Berlanti, Ali Adler and Andrew Kreisberg and executive producer Sarah Schechter envisioned a

contemporary take on the classic DC Comics character—her arc would require her to learn to accept herself to be truly effective. "She's a modern superhero and embraces her powers as well as her insecurities in order to be a successful one," Adler told *EW*, adding, "We're not bound to the history, but we are inspired by it."

↑ J'onn J'onzz at the front of a march for alien rights.

It helped tremendously that Benoist, who had made a name for herself on the high school musical series *Glee* playing wallflower Marley Rose, was such a great fit for the role. The Colorado native landed the part after a rigorous audition process (spanning more than three months), thanks to a winning combination of down-to-earth charm and out-of-this-world charisma. The original Colleen Atwood-designed costume sealed the deal. "It's impossible not to feel empowered when you put it on," Benoist says. "I feel like a different person almost."

In the intervening years Kara remained hopeful even as great change came to National City. For starters *Supergirl* moved from CBS to the CW at the conclusion of its first season. Kara worked with her famous cousin (Tyler Hoechlin), befriended Lex Luthor's half sister Lena (Katie McGrath) and fell for Mon-El (Chris Wood), an alien prince who finds his way to Earth. Kara's horizons also expanded far beyond her home base after she received an interdimensional extrapolator from Team Flash techie Cisco (Carlos Valdes); the device allows her to travel to the primary Arrowverse whenever she wishes to spend time with Flash and the rest of the gang.

Thematically, the drama soared to new heights last season with a topical plot about Supergirl confronting xenophobia toward aliens and divisiveness in the country—which an imprisoned Lex Luthor (Jon Cryer) turns to his advantage. The producers hope to repeat their success by building the upcoming season around another strong, timely theme. "It's our *Black Mirror* season," says Jessica Queller, who was named co-showrunner with

Robert Rovner heading into the series' third season. Rovner adds, "What we're looking at is how technology is impacting the way people engage and giving them an escape to not engage. It speaks to a lot of the stuff the characters will be going through."

To tie in with the weightier subject matter, Supergirl's wardrobe also received a bit of a makeover: The flirty red skirt is gone in favor of some far-more-practical pants. Benoist particularly loves her character's new threads. "I just think it's more adult," she says. Also new this season? Benoist will finally have her name on the director's chair when she steps behind the camera for the first time. "I just felt I'm really drawn to it for a couple seasons now," Benoist says. "Because you know the show so well—and you get to know the character and the world and the tone of the show so well—you can't help but envision certain scenes in a certain way. I want to play with that.

"It's like a chess game, I've realized," she adds. "You move your pawn one way, and then someone knocks your rook down because you can't do a certain stunt you wanted to do. It's all about compromising and trying to be as creative as you can within those boundaries, which is a cool challenge." And as we all know, Benoist is not one to shy away from a challenge. ●

↑ **From top** the arch-villain Lex Luthor (Jon Cryer); Ben Lockwood (Sam Witwer) leads members of the Children of Liberty who are on the wrong side of, well, liberty.

Querl Dox
BRAINIAC 5
JESSE RATH
The genius Coluan was born in the 31st century, where he was a Legion member. In the 21st he's an ally of Kara's and the Superfriends.

Ben Lockwood
AGENT LIBERTY
SAM WITWER
The antialien leader of the Children of Liberty was pardoned for his crimes by a corrupt President—and then jailed for them.

Nia Nal
DREAMER
NICOLE MAINES
The CatCo reporter (and half Naltorian) suited up to help Kara against the Children of Liberty.

Lauren Haley
APRIL PARKER JONES
She's assigned to oversee the D.E.O. by corrupt President Baker, to whom she's initially loyal. When Baker's alliance with Lex is revealed, she has second thoughts.

Eve Teschmacher
ANDREA BROOKS
First Cat's assistant, then Olson's, then Lena's, the intrepid spy was hiding her true allegiance—to Lex—the whole time and is in hiding after his death.

Kelly Olsen
AZIE TESFAI
Olsen's younger sister, the trauma specialist and former military psychiatrist is currently dating Alex Danvers.

Melissa Benoist

IT'S A BIRD . . . IT'S A PLANE . . . IT'S **SUPERGIRL!** THE ACTRESS BEHIND KARA ZOR-EL OPENS UP ABOUT THE LENA LUTHOR DRAMA AND TRYING ON A NEW SUIT IN SEASON 5. BY CHANCELLOR AGARD

Q+A

MUCH LIKE THE MAN BEHIND EVERYONE'S FAVORITE LIGHTNING-fast forensic scientist, actress Melissa Benoist also earned encores on the Fox song-and-dance series *Glee.* (William McKinley High: stealth superhero training school?) And just like Grant Gustin, Benoist has parlayed that theatrical charisma into the role of a bighearted hero we can't help but root for—whether she's in front of or, this season, behind the camera. Benoist gives *EW* a taste of what's to come this year.

Let's start with one of the biggest new developments of the season: You're wearing pants!

MELISSA BENOIST We've been talking about pants since season 1.

Really?

Yes. Every time a writer from the show has come up, and it's freezing cold in Vancouver, I'm like, "Guys, please, can I not wear tights?" I love this. I haven't changed it because it so works, and I think it is very Kara, and I've

PHOTOGRAPHS BY MATTHIAS CLAMER

always felt that, until recently—something's gotta give. Part of my goal in this whole series [is that] I just want there to be a very clear arc for this character—that she evolved as a woman and found her femininity and her adulthood, just a self-discovery.

Season 4 of *Supergirl* was so great—did you feel like the show found another gear?
I do. I think our show has always done well with a little bit of politics. We started wanting to do something super strong and feminist and really talk about strength in women, what that means and how to empower more women. Every day on-set we're thinking about what we want to say to little girls who are watching, and little boys, anyone. We just want to send hope and inclusivity.

Last season really examined Kara's duality: as a reporter and as a superhero. For you, what was it like to get into both sides?
I don't think Clark Kent would be Superman if he didn't have the alter ego and didn't experience what he experiences as a reporter, and the same goes for Kara. What we wanted to talk about this season, and what was important to us, was talking about the power of the press, talking about how they can save the day. The media, when they are really seeking to tell the truth, can change the world and really lessen fear in society. When you shed light on wrongdoings, you can change people's minds.

"I THINK OUR SHOW HAS ALWAYS DONE WELL WITH A LITTLE BIT OF POLITICS"

—MELISSA BENOIST ON ALIEN RIGHTS

The show hewed closely to troubling real-world topics. Was it too much sometimes?
I didn't think that we could've gone too far because it's so scary right now. The world is really stressful.... A lot of our [viewers are] younger, and I don't want people to lose that sense of hope right now, even though the world is a very stressful place. That really is what Supergirl fights for in general: hope, help and compassion.

The end of season 4 saw Lena Luthor finding out that Kara is Supergirl. What was it like to get to that, to read that in the script?
I knew it was coming, and I knew it was going to happen, but I didn't know how they were going to do it. I was devastated that it was Lex Luthor that told her. I mean, that was just such a shot in the heart to Lena, a character that my character loves so dearly. It was painful. I think this season's going to be... I've been told it's going to be a fight for Lena's soul, essentially. That's such a classic, in the Superman mythology. You know, they were friends first. Lex and Clark are friends first. I know that's how it is in the comic books too. I don't know if they explore that with Lena and Supergirl in the comics.... She is going to kill everything they write for her this season. It's painful, but I think it's going to be a really fulfilling story to tell.

→ **Opposite, from left** Chyler Leigh, Melissa Benoist and David Harewood.

↓ Supergirl (Benoist) with President Olivia Marsdin (Lynda Carter).

All Dolled

REJECTED THREADS
Winn's first design for Kara was far from a hit. "I wouldn't even wear it to the beach," she says. But the look (complete with a red headband) wasn't that far off from her 1970s garb: hot pants, puffy sleeves and ballerina slippers.

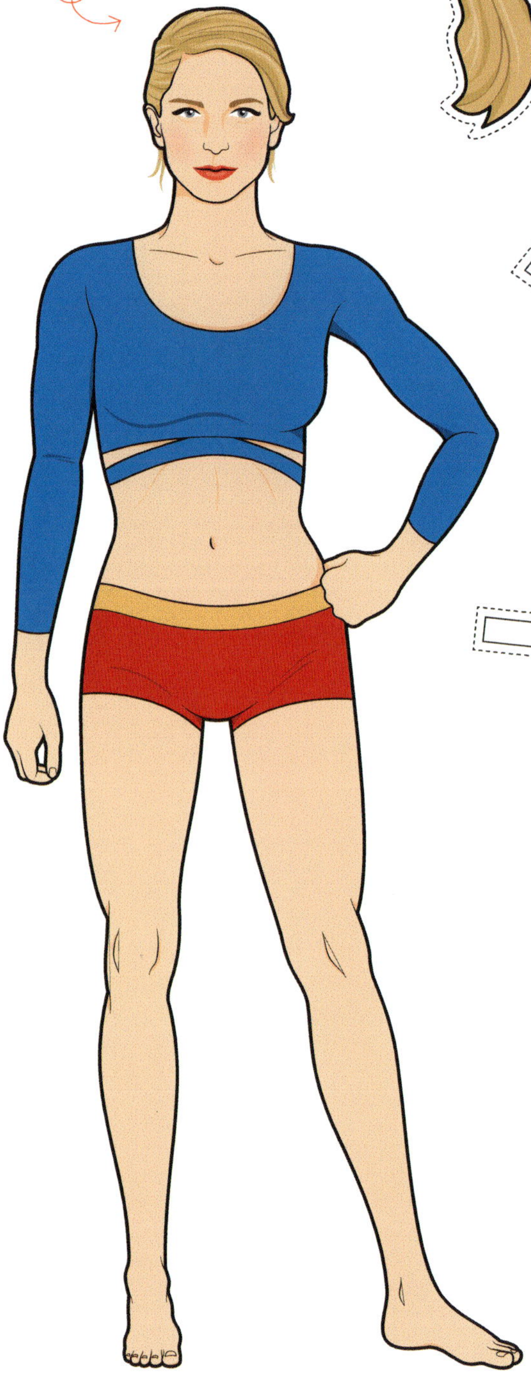

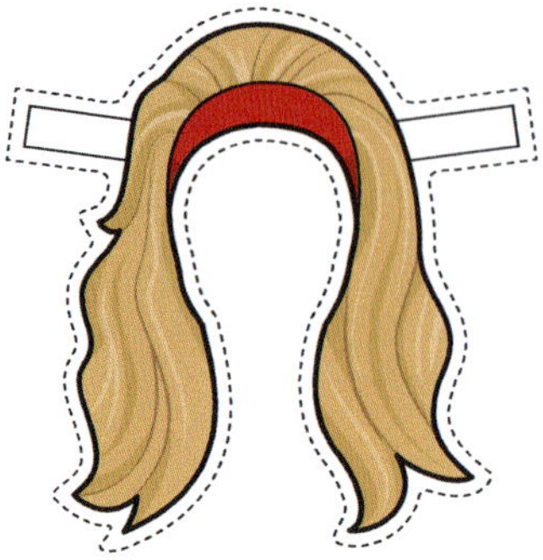

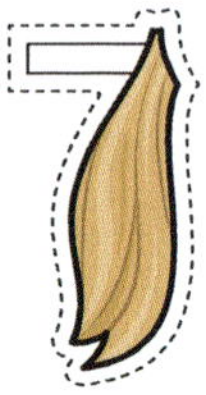

REPORTER, UNDERCOVER
As a reporter at CatCo, Kara rocks a series of plaid skirts, business-casual shirts and knee-length dresses, but the most important parts of her disguise are glasses and a so-sensible ponytail.

ALTERNATE HISTORY
When the costume designers selected these Dr. Martens for Kara's second suit, they looked at a different iteration of Supergirl (Kara Kent/Kara In-Ze, who sported red lace-up boots) for inspiration.

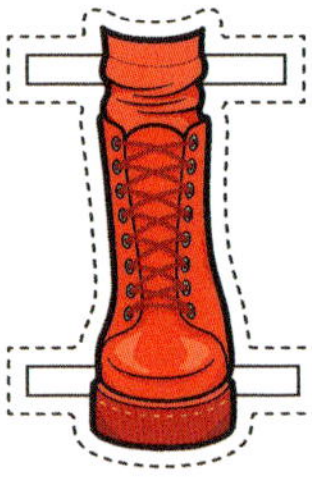

ILLUSTRATIONS BY BROWN BIRD DESIGN

Up

All of Kara's costumes over five seasons (yes, even those pants) have lifted inspiration from her **COMIC-BOOK** roots. BY ALYSSA SMITH

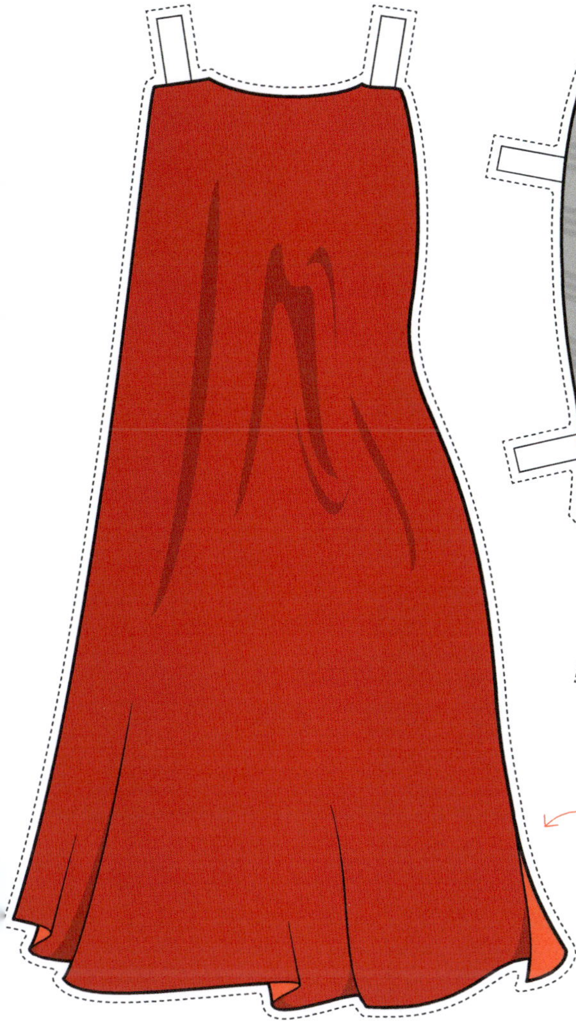

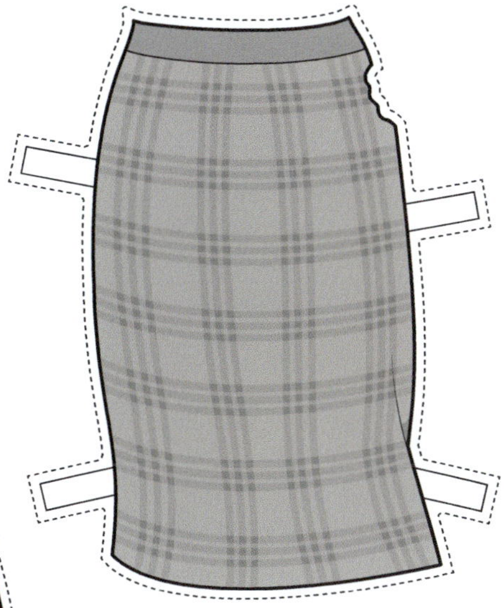

THE CAPE HELPS WITH AERODYNAMICS
Who knew? (Superman, obv.)

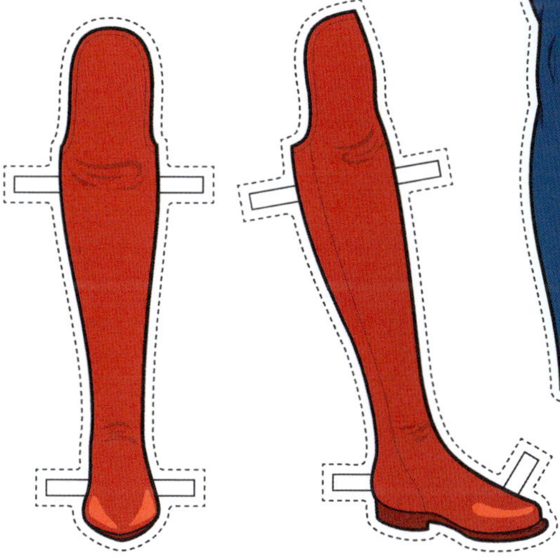

IT'S NOT AN 'S'
Supergirl's long-sleeve blue shirt and skirt (later changed to red) and wedge heels have sported the House of El insignia since her first appearance in 1959's *Action Comics* #252.

FLYING BY THE SEAT OF...
Kara's new pants! Kara Zor-El has worn pants many times in her comic history, including a tie-in comic to *Smallville*, and in multiple versions of the video game Injustice.

The Lege

NDS Are True

THE CW'S BAND OF LOVABLE SCREWUPS DEFEND HISTORY FROM A SERIES OF INCREASINGLY WACKY THREATS. HERE'S HOW THEY ACCOMPLISH IT ALL. BY RICH SANDS • PHOTOGRAPHS BY CARLOS SERRAO

OUTCASTS. MISFITS. EXPENDABLES. B-LIST SUPERHEROES. These are some of the many self-deprecating ways the characters of *DC's Legends of Tomorrow* have described themselves over the years. And the least celebrated member of the Arrowverse wears its outsider status as a badge of honor. "We don't play it safe," says cast member Caity Lotz. "The show isn't a traditional, 'Let's figure out how to package this and sell it to the masses' [format]. I feel like it's really authentic and original. There's not really another show that's like it."

Legends was cobbled together with a group of secondary DC Comics characters who had first appeared in *Arrow* and *The Flash.* The massive ensemble was then recruited onto a time-traveling ship, the *Waverider,* by the enigmatic Rip Hunter (Arthur Darvill). Their mission: to stop the immortal warlord Vandal Savage from conquering the world in the year 2166. Hunter eventually was forced to confess the truth: "I chose you all because 100 years from now your lives have minimal effect on the recorded timeline." Ouch.

← **Clockwise from left** The Legends take Woodstock; Leonard Snart (Wentworth Miller) and Rip Hunter (Arthur Darvill) in season 1; Firestorm buds Martin Stein (Victor Garber) and Jefferson "Jax" Jackson (Franz Drameh) consult with Sara Lance (Caity Lotz); Rip with Mick Rory (Dominic Purcell) and Nate Heywood (Nick Zano).

Who's Who on the *Waverider*

THE LEGENDS USE THEIR TIMESHIP AS A MOBILE-OPERATIONS BASE WITH HUGE HELP FROM ITS A.I., GIDEON (AMY LOUISE PEMBERTON).

BY ALYSSA SMITH

Rip Hunter

ARTHUR DARVILL

The ship's original captain, rogue agent of the Time Masters and founder of the Time Bureau met his eventual end while battling the time demon Mallus.

Sara Lance

WHITE CANARY

CAITY LOTZ

The *Waverider*'s second captain and expert tactician is a former member of both the League of Assassins and Team Arrow; she's currently dating the former director of the Time Bureau Ava.

Ray Palmer

THE ATOM

BRANDON ROUTH

The genius founder of Palmer Technologies created a supersuit bestowing incredible shrinking abilities. Before joining the Legends, Ray used the suit to support both Team Arrow and Team Flash.

Martin Stein and Jefferson 'Jax' Jackson

FIRESTORM

VICTOR GARBER AND FRANZ DRAMEH

The two, together, once created the nuclear-powered Firestorm. While their relationship started off rocky, the two grew to love each other. After Stein's death, Jax left the Legends.

↑ **Clockwise from top** In "The Magnificent Eight," the Legends first meet Johnathon Schaech's Jonah Hex (pictured second from left); Nate and Amaya Jiwe (Maisie Richardson-Sellers), in happier times; Damien Darhk (Neal McDonough) and Malcolm Merlyn (John Barrowman), two members of the Legion of Doom.

The original rag-tag team included Sara Lance (Lotz), the crime-fighting vigilante White Canary; Ray Palmer (Brandon Routh), the Atom, an incredible shrinking superhero; physicist Martin Stein (Victor Garber) and auto mechanic Jefferson "Jax" Jackson (Franz Drameh), together the hero Firestorm; Mick Rory and Leonard Snart (Dominic Purcell and Wentworth Miller), literal partners in crime Heat Wave and Captain Cold; and star-crossed lovers Kendra Saunders (Ciara Renée) and Carter Hall (Falk Hentschel), Hawkgirl and Hawkman.

Despite an intriguing premise, *Legends* struggled to find a clear voice when it debuted in early 2016. The plot involved a series of adventures throughout history, and while there were brief, heartfelt moments featuring each character's quest for redemption, the show (at first) took itself a little too seriously. "When I was writing those early episodes, all I really knew were the characters' superpowers," says executive producer Phil Klemmer, who was hired after the CW had picked up the series.

The network decided to give the show a second season, and

Kendra Saunders and Scythian Torvil

HAWKGIRL AND HAWKMAN

CIARA RENEE AND FALK HENTSCHEL

The two eternally reincarnated lovers helped to take down Vandal Savage but then left.

Mick Rory

HEAT WAVE

DOMINIC PURCELL

The hotheaded former criminal moonlights as the bestselling romance author Rebecca Silver.

Leonard Snart

CAPTAIN COLD

WENTWORTH MILLER

Heat Wave's partner in crime came to embrace the Legends' cause—and sacrificed himself to save their lives.

Nate Heywood

STEEL

NICK ZANO

After rescuing all of the Legends from where they are stranded in time, the historian joins the team—and picks up a superpower along the way, thanks to Ray.

Amaya Jiwe

VIXEN

MAISIE RICHARDSON-SELLERS

A totem-wielder and protector of her African village, after helping the Legends defeat Mallus, she returns to Zambesi.

Nora Darhk

COURTNEY FORD

The daughter of Damien Darhk, the once-vessel of Mallus, and current Time Bureau agent has an "it's complicated" relationship with the Legends.

Zari Tomaz

TALA ASHE

The antigovernment hacker and wielder of the Air Totem hails from a dystopian future timeline of 2042 that was destroyed after the events of season 4, which also erased this version of Z from existence.

Ava Sharpe

JES MACALLAN

The director of the Time Bureau discovers she's a clone—thanks, 2213!—but even more shocked to find she's the 12th incarnation at the Bureau.

Gary Green

AGENT 1066

ADAM TSEKHMAN

Once, just an intern.

John Constantine

MATT RYAN

A warlock and demonologist, he has skills that come in handy after magical creatures escape their prison, including a man-eating unicorn, a fairy godmother and a musical Minotaur.

Charlie

MAISIE RICHARDSON-SELLERS

The shape-shifter is stuck in this form after Constantine's spell. Despite that rough start, after being trapped in a time loop, she's come to terms with being a Legend.

Mona Wu

RAMONA YOUNG

After joining the Time Bureau as their official magical-creature handler, she falls for one of the creatures, a Kaupe, who accidentally scratches her and infects her with Kaupe DNA.

↑ Charlie and Sara, right before the show's Bollywood number

Legends 2.0 quickly earned a reputation for taking outrageous swings, including one trip to 17th-century France to ensure that King Louis XIII consummated his marriage and another to 1979 to save college student Barack Obama from a telepathic gorilla. Executive producer Keto Shimizu, who joined the show from *Arrow* in season 2, worked with Klemmer to develop a more lighthearted attitude toward the band of time-traveling heroes. "I thought creatively the show should be more about the humor and the time periods and dysfunctional family dynamic," she says.

The delightful madness continued with the introduction of Beebo, an adorable Muppet-like toy from the 1990s that nearly inspired the Vikings to conquer North America—plus run-ins with vicious unicorns, fairy godmothers and lucha libre wrestlers. "You get to a point where you can just drop these characters into a Bollywood scene," says Klemmer, referencing an actual episode. "They feel like gimmicks or gags, but the conceit of the original show was so preposterous that it could withstand it once you know the characters."

Since those characters are less

↑ **From top**
Ray Palmer (Brandon Routh) under attack by a spirit-possessed puppet; Viking shieldmaiden Freydis (Katia Winter) with her new god Beebo.

widely known than Green Arrow, the Flash and Supergirl, the writers recognized they could get away with more. "We think of ourselves more of a comedy with really strong character moments," executive producer Grainne Godfree says. "The thing we talk about is how can we be more subversive, how can we be more poignant, [and] how can we be more fun, because we love all three of those elements at the same time."

The cast embraced the changes. "It's fun to play the comedy instead of being so dark and tortured all of the time," says Lotz, whose character has emerged as the team's leader. "This Sara gets to have a lot more fun."

Legends has also had something of a revolving door with cast members coming and going over the years. When season 5 begins in January, only Lotz, Purcell, Routh and Amy Louise Pemberton (the voice and occasional persona of Gideon, the *Waverider's* artificial intelligence) will remain from the original roster, replaced by newcomers like demon-fighting warlock John Constantine (Matt Ryan, resurrected from his short-lived NBC series).

Critics have begun to take notice of the show's go-for-broke storytelling and inclusive cast (in addition to a racially diverse ensemble, *Legends* has also prominently featured LGBTQ themes and Muslim and Jewish characters). "I feel like in this day and age it would be nice, particularly for young people, to have a show that feel like a respite from the news of the world," Godfree says. "And also it's about a very disparate group of people that can show a little bit of a road map of how we can all be together."

The new season will continue the trend of cast turnover. Thanks to a change in the timeline triggered in the season 4 finale, mystically powered hacker Zari Tomaz (Tala Ashe) is no longer (and has never been) on the team, replaced by her brother Behrad (Shayan Sobhian). "We will see Zari again as someone who's lived a very different life than she had in the original timeline," Shimizu promises. "It creates some fun dynamics with members of our team."

And, in news that shocked longtime *Legends* fans, it was announced in August that Ray and Nora (the demonic minion turned unlikely ally played by Courtney Ford) will depart this season, following their surprising romance. (Routh and Ford are married in real life.) "We really felt like this was the right way and the right time to bring this story to a close," Shimizu says, without revealing the specifics of their exit.

She promises that the story "sends them off in a way that is not a closed door. There are so many characters who never truly leave the show. We don't like to kill characters; we like to let them go off and evolve for a bit, and then we revisit them." ●

ADDITIONAL REPORTING > CHANCELLOR AGARD

A Super Ensemble

THE CAST OF DC'S LEGENDS OF TOMORROW MANAGE TO MAKE TRAVELING THROUGH TIME LOOK EASY—AND WHILE DOING SO, CHEW AS MUCH SCENERY AS POSSIBLE. BY CHANCELLOR AGARD

Q+A

WHEN THE *LEGENDS* CAST READ THEIR SCRIPTS, THEY OFTEN CAN'T quite believe what their time-traveling counterparts will be up to this time. "[We can] go from a killer unicorn to a fairy godmother in one episode," marvels Matt Ryan (Constantine). In September 2019, seven of the ensemble talked about their first experiences together, their hopes for the *Legends* future, why the Tickle-Me-Elmo-inspired toy Beebo has become the show's mascot—and how lucky they are to be able to portray the crew of the *Waverider*.

↑ **Clockwise from top left** Maisie Richardson-Sellers, Courtney Ford, Matt Ryan, Jes Macallan, Tala Ashe, Dominic Purcell, Caity Lotz, Nick Zano, and Brandon Routh

Do you remember the first time you met?

CAITY LOTZ I remember Brandon asking me, "How is it over on *Arrow*? Do you like it over there?" I guess we've known each other for a while. The whole cast didn't really get together until Comic-Con, right?

BRANDON ROUTH We had dinner. Arthur [Darvill] and Ciara [Renée] in Vancouver.

LOTZ Your memory is better than mine. I just remember Dom being on the carpet at, like, the upfront, like, doing interviews. And he was like, "Yeah, I'm on this new show, *Legends of the Fall*." And I'm like, "No, it's *Legends of Tomorrow*." [*Laughs*]

DOMINIC PURCELL I do remember saying that. Yeah... it was very sudden. I did a guest-star [appearance] with Wentworth [Miller] on *The Flash*. Obviously the chemistry between me and Wentworth is really cool. Before I knew it, I was doing *Legends of Tomorrow* with Wentworth and the cast. [*Laughs*] "*Legends of the Fall*." That's very typical of me. That's the kind of stupid stuff I say all the time.

ROUTH The first season was challenging because we were trying to find our legs and understand what kind of show we really were. I mean, we had a strong blueprint, but we'd never shot a pilot.

> **"THESE PEOPLE ARE MY FAMILY, AND IT'S A STRANGE, STRANGE FAMILY, BUT THIS IS IT"**
>
> —TALA ASHE ON EMBRACING HER *LEGENDS* CASTMATES

What was it like for those of you who joined the show after its first season, to step onto a show that was already going?

NICK ZANO I came on season 2. Tala, you were 3?

TALA ASHE Mm-hm. Matt was 4.

MATT RYAN I did a couple episodes in 3, and then in 4 I became a regular.

ZANO When I got there, they were coming off a season that [had] a vibe and a tone that they were trying to change. That was very difficult. Nobody knew what was happening, what the agenda was and what we were going to become. Season 2 was a transition year of saying, we are not the show, but grow with us, because we're going somewhere.

ASHE Totally. Matt, you've had a seamless entry. Maybe internally it didn't feel that way, but... for me it was really hard. I think it also taps into my own insecurities about social situations. It took most of season 3, really, for me to feel like I was part of a team, onscreen and off. It wasn't until the "Groundhog Day" episode [where] what that episode asked of me was of vulnerability. I couldn't hide after or during that episode. After that, I felt... these people are my family, and it's a strange, strange family, but this is it. I love them. Everybody was so supportive.

MAISIE RICHARDSON-SELLERS On my first day on-set, I was in a basement in this abandoned mental-asylum hospital, and it was just me and Brandon, and we were chained to a chair, and the chains are really hard to get on and off, so they just kind of left them on between [scenes]. It was dark, dank, and I was like, "Well, this is my way to arrive." [*Laughs*] But from then on, it was great. Thank goodness I had Nick. We arrived at the same time, so we had the opportunity to be the new kids on the block.

↓ Sara Lance (Caity Lotz) faces off against Caesar in season 3's opening episode. At right: Lotz in 2017.

↑ Maisie Richardson-Sellers in 2018 (left). Matt Ryan in 2018 (right).

What has been your most memorable experience so far?

LOTZ Fighting Julius Caesar on the beach was pretty fun. It was like summertime, and it was just nice to be out on the beach too. And, yeah, directing this season has been just such a cool, cool experience.

RYAN I would say that I think Nick's most memorable moment was when I was doing naked yoga.

ASHE [*Laughs*] Also mine.

RYAN Also yours.

ZANO Here's a little behind-the-scenes fact: Matt actually rehearsed yoga [*laughs*] for that scene. Someone actually taught him poses. So he spent time in choreography doing naked-yoga scenes.

RYAN Yeah. I spent a lot of time learning naked Tai Chi and then the only thing that was in the shots was a back stretch.

ZANO Well, for me, one day that like really sticks out is the day we got to wear everybody else's hero costumes. When you're on the *Legends'* set, and Caity is Supergirl and I'm Arrow and Adam [Tsekhman] is the Flash, we just felt like we were the tiny siblings who snuck into the big sibling's closet to play dress-up. [*Laughs*]

Are you surprised by how much the show has evolved?

PURCELL Yeah, totally. All of us were completely surprised by that because, as I said, the first season really wasn't something that was working, and now it is. Now I love the show. The critics love it. The fans love it. I love it. The cast love it. You can tell how much fun we're having on the show, and I think that's why it has become so successful.

LOTZ I think the whole show had to find its voice and what exactly it was. Now it just feels like what it always was and what it's always been.

RYAN You can literally throw any different characters into the mix and get a different dynamic and then find a new story from that. Even if it's a character that's been established in a different universe or in a different comic book, like Constantine, that's never been written before. It's new, you know. We're just discovering stuff the whole while.

What has been some of the most challenging days on-set?

ASHE Last year it was the finale episode at Heyworld. I had to hold Nick Zano's body in my arms while the Legends formed a circle around me, and there were chupacabra and cocker spaniel things coming toward me, and we had to sing a James Taylor song, and I was weeping. That was the hardest day for me.

↑ Tala Ashe in 2018 (left). Nick Zano in 2018 (right).

ZANO As awkward and clunky as it was, I remember watching that last scene with my mom in my house, and my mom and I welled up. Watching it made me very emotional. Damn, if they're not magicians putting our show together to make it great.

When you first got to Beebo in the script, what was it like to read that the thing that's going to save everyone at the end of your TV season is going to be a big, fluffy, cuddly toy?

ZANO I thought that was it. I was like, we were onto something and we just wrote a grenade into our own house. I was going to say, no way that this works or is believable in any sense. And I was 1,000 percent wrong. So ever since then I always give it a grain of salt and trust the system.

ASHE Yeah. I think what's happened is in this dysfunctional family of ours, we've developed trust between us and our crew and the writers and the directors where we're all sort of willing to go for the ride now, which is really lovely.

PURCELL I remember exactly what I said. "Okay, this is a career-ender." [*Laughs*] "This is the end of my career for sure." I mean, seriously, that's what I thought. "Okay, I'm never coming back from this." But again, in time, that kind of stuff belongs on *Legends*, and we are allowed basically to do whatever we want. That's the beauty of this show.

Let's talk about what you remember about last season's "Legends of To-Meow-Meow," where you were messing with the timeline.

ZANO When I first read the script, I read the full episode, and I texted [showrunner] Phil [Klemmer], and I was like, "Phil, this may be the best episode we have ever done ever if we do it within the script." We all went for it. We had puppets, we were in recording studios singing kids' theme songs. Like, Tala was a cat. It was a doggone free-for-all.

RYAN The line that I say when I walk in and see the puppets and I say, "What the 'bleep'?" I mean, that was real. I was like, what were we doing? I turned up on the show coming from doing Constantine as a drama. And then on one of my first or second days…it was when you guys were being attacked by the unicorn and you were on acid. So I'm walking along, like, "Oh my God, what is this show?" I've never done anything where I've been so excited to see a script, because you just don't know what genre it's going to be.

ASHE Once we did the "Groundhog Day" episode and it worked,

I think that allowed the writers' room to do these sort of high-concept or alternate-concept episodes. Those are the ones that I've been really excited to read.
RICHARDSON-SELLERS So many people when they go to conventions come up and they talk about Beebo. That was taking a big risk, and when I read it on paper, I was like, this is ridiculous. But then when you see it come to life, it's wonderfully, hilariously ridiculous and it just works.
ASHE Speaking for myself, and I think you guys would agree, I feel really lucky to be part of something that takes risks because we could very easily be a procedural, and there's a lot of procedurals that do very well on television. What I'm interested in, being an artist and an actor, is a challenge; doing things that stretch you and challenge you.

Maisie, you're now portraying a second, completely different character. What has it been like for you to play two separate characters on the show?
RICHARDSON-SELLERS As an actress it's the most beautiful gift, because I love reinventing and transforming characters and exploring different worlds. I don't think the two could be more different. Amaya Jiwe was very straitlaced, very professional and had a lot at stake constantly. To be able to play the complete opposite in Charlie, who is someone who's got a happy-go-lucky, in-it-for-the-ride, adventurous, wild-child [attitude] has been brilliant. And I think this season we finally get to see some of Charlie's backstory [and] why she's the way she is. It's actually quite a tragic and dark story. She's going to pal with people you wouldn't quite expect. Everyone has their darkness and their light.

"I'M DOING MY BEST NOT TO TAKE THESE LAST FEW EPISODES FOR GRANTED"

—BRANDON ROUTH ON HIS DEPARTURE FROM *LEGENDS*

Caity, Brandon, back in *Arrow*, did you ever expect that you would go on to play your characters for almost 100 episodes?
LOTZ I mean, it's pretty wild. Just on *Arrow* alone, Sara's journey was huge. Such a big arc. Coming over to *Legends*, it was hard when we first started because you get a sense of what your character would say and who they are, and then all of a sudden on *Legends*, Sara's cracking jokes. On *Arrow*, everything was so dark, and then I was like, "What? I would never say that. Sara would never say that." Trying to find the balance of fitting into this new show but still making it feel like Sara Lance was a bit of a challenge.
ROUTH It was no guarantee [Ray] was even gonna make it [through] the length of the season. They had a plan for him, but it just kind of depended on how everybody meshed together.

↓ The *Legends'* season 4 finale "Hey, World!"

The news broke that your character is leaving the show, Brandon. How are you feeling about the end of the road approaching?
ROUTH It's been challenging. I am doing my best to not take these last few episodes for granted but really cherishing my awesome cast and crew that I've had the opportunity to work with for the last five years. I'll miss the back-and-forth with Ray and Nora, the bromance of Nate and Ray. I'll miss the representation that fans get, the different aspects that

people love about Ray, whether it's his eternal optimism and showing people that it's okay to be happy and find light [or how] to find the balance in their own lives. There's so many things that Ray brings to the ship. You know, my life models Ray's quite a bit in my energy. I'm very similar to Ray in many ways. His journey is my journey and vice versa.

What was it like to have Caity as a director this year?

RYAN I love it. I came off that [set] last night, we were there, like, 14 hours. Over the time Caity was directing this episode, apart from all of the other amazing [things] that she's done, she gave me like two, maybe three or four, really performance-changing notes that literally took me in a direction, which was amazing. I said to her, I was just like, Oh my God.

RICHARDSON-SELLERS Yeah, she killed it. We're always sort of rushing, but she really took the time to make sure that we rehearsed, to make sure everybody was comfortable with the arc of every scene. She took that time to really focus on the acting, which is a luxury in episodic TV, especially network TV. She's crushed it. She just wants to reinvent and leaned into the stylistic aspect of her episode. We're doing shots that personally I've never done on episodic TV before. It takes a lot of confidence to take those risks. I can't wait to see how it turns out.

Is there more pressure now because of how much fans love the show?

RICHARDSON-SELLERS If anything, any pressure is to trust. Like just trust the show.

ZANO I have found myself saying after takes, "God damn it, I love our show," out loud. Like, I love our show. We started early with this show—we had a "no a--hole" policy. No one was allowed to be an a--hole. And in our cast, there was no cockiness; we were one unit making this amazing show that we're all super proud to be a part of and continue to be part of its evolution.

LOTZ I think at this point we've really earned the trust of the network and the studio. Our show's always been really risky, and it does weird things and takes chances, and if you take that away, then you take what makes *Legends Legends.*

Is the willingness to take risks the secret ingredient that makes *Legends* work?

LOTZ We've got nothing to lose. So let's do it. ●

THIS INTERVIEW HAS BEEN EDITED AND CONDENSED FOR CLARITY

↑ Brandon Routh in 2019 (left). Dominic Purcell in 2019 (right).

A Not-So-Accurate Time M

1 South Dakota
70 MILLION B.C.

When the *Waverider* crash-lands in the Cretaceous period, the team encounters a grumpy Tyrannosaurus rex that Ray names **Gertrude.**

43.9695°N, 99.9018°W

2 Woodstock
1969

Jerry Garcia's saliva, Jimi Hendrix's pendant and a strand of Janis Joplin's hair are the psychedelic ingredients the team collects for Constantine's spell to stop a carnivorous **unicorn.**

42.0409° N, 74.1182° W

3 Hollywood
1967

After a twentysomething **George Lucas** is nearly killed by the Legion of Doom, the Legends must persuade the aspiring filmmaker not to give up his dreams.

34.0928° N, 118.3287° W

4 Memphis
1954

The Legends are all shook up when they must help **Elvis Presley** cut a demo record with a guitar that's haunted by the mysterious Death Totem and has the power to raise the spirits of the dead.

35.1495°N, 90.0490°W

5 Vinland
1000 A.D.

A young Martin Stein is teleported to the New World with 1992's hottest toy, the adorable talking **Cuddle Me Beebo.** The fluffy blue doll is soon embraced as a new Viking god.

51.5964° N, 55.5334° W

ILLUSTRATIONS BY MARTIN GEE

ap

The Legends have tracked down magical beings, malevolent time deities and historical anachronisms across the globe. Here's a snapshot of some of our favorite missions. BY RICH SANDS

6 Bath, England
1802

While attempting to keep **Jane Austen**'s writing career on track, the squad meets a man imbued with the powers of the seductive Hindu god of love. There's a Bollywood-style musical number.

51.3811°N, 2.3590°W

7 London
2166

In this dystopian future, the immortal tyrant **Vandal Savage** murders Rip Hunter's family as his quest for world domination is about to come to fruition.

51.5074°N, 0.1278°W

8 Camelot
507 A.D.

The Legends' quest to protect the Spear of Destiny leads them to Camelot, where they fight alongside the Knights of the Round Table. Sara steals a passionate goodbye kiss with **Queen Guinevere.**

53.6458° N, 1.7850° W

9 Paris
1927

Ernest Hemingway, Salvador Dalí and F. Scott Fitzgerald are unintentionally drawn into a mission to find the magically displaced **Minotaur.**

48.8566°N, 2.3522°E

10 Cisalpine Gaul
49 B.C.

The Legends return **Julius Caesar** from an anachronistic displacement in Aruba in 2017 but, in classic fashion, inadvertently show the Roman ruler a path toward conquering the entire world.

45.7640° N, 4.8357° E

BaTW

OMAN Begins

MEET THE NEWEST CAPED CRUSADER JOINING THE ARROWVERSE'S RANKS. HERE'S WHY RUBY ROSE'S BATWOMAN IS THE HERO WE NEED AND DESERVE. BY GINA McINTYRE • PHOTOGRAPHS BY CARLOS SERRAO

M

MOVE OVER, BRUCE WAYNE. THERE'S a new hero in Gotham, and she's pretty freaking formidable. "Batwoman is the only caped crusader in town," explains Caroline Dries, the showrunner tasked with bringing the exploits of Kate Kane, aka Batwoman, to the screen. "She's a really courageous, no bulls--- badass who knows herself very well and is not afraid of sharing that with the world."

Batwoman and her badass antics made their series debut on Oct. 6, becoming the first live-action show ever to center on an out-LGBTQ superhero. Anchoring the CW series is Australian model-turned-actress Ruby Rose (*Orange Is the New Black*), who first appeared as the character in 2018's "Elseworlds" crossover event.

Being a part of a superensemble was a new experience for Rose, but even then, there was something remarkably powerful about playing the character. That feeling has only intensified now that Kate is battling bad guys on her own. "When I put that suit on, everything kind of changes and you feel a shift in your energy," she says.

With *Batwoman,* the CW is shifting its superenergy in a different direction, adopting the seriously gritty aesthetic traditionally associated with the Dark Knight. When the show opens, Batman's been missing for three years, leaving Gotham overrun by criminals; Jacob Kane (Dougray Scott), head of Crows Private Security, now protects the city. After he becomes the target of the Alice in Wonderland gang—led by the unhinged Alice (*Reign*'s Rachel Skarsten)—his estranged daughter Kate picks up the absent vigilante's mantle.

"It's a bit of a shell shock for Kate to return to Gotham, the city that she loved and was raised in—I don't think she anticipated to come back to this city that's falling apart," Rose says.

Kate uses the skills she picked up at military school and years of brutal survival training to clean up the streets of her hometown, encountering plenty of villains along the way. Dries says audiences

← **Clockwise from left** Kate Kane (Ruby Rose) discusses upgrades with Luke Fox (Camrus Johnson); Rachel Skarsten's Alice; Kate and ex Sophie (Meagan Tandy) in happier times.

Who's Who in Batwoman's Gotham

BATMAN HAS BEEN MISSING FOR YEARS, AND IN HIS ABSENCE, THE CITY HAS BECOME A DIFFERENT PLACE. *BY ALYSSA SMITH*

Kate Kane

BATWOMAN

RUBY ROSE

The Australian model's first major Hollywood role was in Netflix's *Orange Is the New Black*. In the 'verse, her Kate Kane (Bruce Wayne's rule-breaking cousin) joined Arrow, Supergirl and the Flash in the 2018 crossover "Elseworlds."

Sophie Moore

MEAGAN TANDY

Her kidnapping at the hands of the Wonderland Gang brings Kate Kane back to Gotham. Moore portrays Kane's ex-girlfriend and Crows agent. She has previously had roles on the CW's *Teen Wolf* and *Charmed* and Lifetime's reality show drama *UnREAL*.

Luke Fox

CAMRUS JOHNSON

As the protector of the Batcave (and son of Wayne's R&D director Lucius Fox), he's kept Batman's secret for a while—but he is willing to open the vaults for the city's newest protector. This isn't Johnson's first hero franchise; he appeared in Netflix's *Luke Cage*.

↑ **Clockwise from top** Kate in action; Sophie in the hands of the Wonderland Gang; Alice and Batwoman get physical.

should expect intense run-ins with Alice—the series' answer to the Joker—as well as a rogues' gallery of Batman foes. "In episode 3, we have a pretty serious *Batman* villain show up thinking, 'I'm going to f---ing kill Batman,'" she says.

But Kate's wrestling with more personal matters too. She's never quite recovered from the profoundly painful loss of her mother and sister, who were killed years earlier. She's also still carrying a serious torch for her ex-girlfriend Sophie (Meagan Tandy), who was one of her father's top officers. "She's heavy," Rose says. "She has a really heavy heart for a lot of very valid reasons."

And while Kate is a committed loner, she does also have an emotional and tactical support system in the form of compassionate stepsister Mary (Nicole Kang) and crafty Luke Fox (Camrus Johnson), son of Wayne Enterprises' tech guru Lucius Fox.

Although the character of Batwoman has been around in at least some form since 1956, creators are hoping that this modern incarnation will offer something entirely new within the framework of familiar mythology. "The thing for me that's so exciting about Batwoman is really her fierceness, you know?" says executive producer Sarah Schechter. "Especially as embodied by Ruby, there's something so challenging and, to me, exciting about a woman who is unapologetic about her strength." ●

ADDITIONAL REPORTING > CHANCELLOR AGARD

Mary Hamilton

NICOLE KANG

Kate may not always get along with her stepsister, but the pair share at least two common bonds: their love for Gotham and a strong sense of justice. It's Mary who lets Kate know when her ex gets kidnapped.

Jacob Kane

DOUGRAY SCOTT

Veteran actor Scott (*Ever After, Hemlock Grove*) joins the cast as Kate Kane's estranged father and leader of Crows Security, a paramilitary force created after Batman goes missing and leaves Gotham unprotected.

Catherine Hamilton-Kane

ELIZABETH ANWEIS

Kate's stepmother Catherine (played by Anweis, known recently for *Twin Peaks: The Return* and *9-1-1*) is a self-made billionaire who sees the emergence of a brand-new vigilante as bad for business—in particular, hers.

Alice

RACHEL SKARSTEN

Every hero needs a heel, and in Gotham's world the crazier they are, the more supporters flock to their banner. Skarsten (*Reign, Lost Girl*) portrays that villain: Alice, the manic leader of the Wonderland Gang, who has a secret connection to Kate's past.

Ruby Rose

CUE THE BAT-SIGNAL: THE ARROWVERSE'S NEWEST HERO SUITS UP AND SPILLS ABOUT HER FIRST DAYS ON-SET AND WHAT TO EXPECT FROM BATWOMAN.

BY CHANCELLOR AGARD

Q+A

RUBY ROSE IS ON THE OTHER SIDE OF THE LAW now. The 33-year-old Australian actress and model first made a splash stateside playing Litchfield Penitentiary inmate Stella Carlin in the third season of Netflix's *Orange Is the New Black*. But for her latest role, Rose is trading in a life of crime for a life of crime-fighting to play Kate Kane—otherwise known as Batwoman. *EW* talked with Rose about her move to Gotham and finding her character through one impeccably designed suit.

Take us back to the first week of finally getting to film *Batwoman*. What was the best part for you?

RUBY ROSE I would say just getting to read the episode and see where it's going to take off. Because the pilot was a lot of explaining Kate Kane's past and going through a lot of her trauma and a lot of the baggage and fights that she's had to prevail through—and personal things—and discovering how she kind of gets to go back to Gotham and essentially put on the bat suit. But now that we're getting into some [further] episodes, we're really discovering more about all the characters as well and their layers and their reasoning. And that part's been really fascinating.

PHOTOGRAPH BY CARTER SMITH

What's been your favorite gadget so far?
The suit. Colleen Atwood is brilliant at designing, but she also puts her heart and soul into it. And you really feel it, and you're there every step of the process of making tweaks and even just fittings and changing things for comfort or changing things for the aesthetics, and you really feel like you've helped create this suit. So it's got a very personal feeling when you put it on.

A lot has been made of Batwoman's being the first openly gay lead character on a superhero show. Does that come with extra pressure?
Not really. I mean, I don't really take any of the external parts [into account]. When I go to work, I'm really just thinking about what's happening that day in the scene and how to bring truth to it. But I do feel elated, and I feel really thrilled and excited and happy that we're at a place that we do have an openly gay superhero. And also this is a superhero that's never been played before. And that, to me, is also wildly... I feel literally out of words.

What do you hope the audience takes away from watching *Batwoman*?
I think that there's a really good balance between humor and groundedness. Like, these characters are just very 2019 or 2020 or whatever. So that's been fun. I think that there's also a really good mix of characters with different traits that kind of offset some of the more traumatic parts or some of the more [violent]—not that it's super violent, but it's definitely not *not* violent. I just think there's the perfect balance of everything you need to

→ **Clockwise from left:** Nicole Kang, Dougray Scott, Ruby Rose, Meagan Tandy, Rachel Skarsten, Camrus Johnson and Elizabeth Anweis.

"I FEEL REALLY THRILLED AND EXCITED AND HAPPY THAT WE'RE AT A PLACE THAT WE DO HAVE AN OPENLY GAY SUPERHERO"
—RUBY ROSE ON HER CAPED CRUSADER

← Batwoman (Rose) in her pilot episode.

kind of walk away from every episode feeling more full—whoever you're rooting for, because you could be rooting for a number of people. I think it's going to be really easy and very interesting to see who becomes fan favorites. Take Batwoman out of it, and it's like... People have their favorite character, and it's for different reasons in who they relate to and who they identify with. I'm interested to see how that pans out.

Behind the Super Scenes

Saving the world week in and week out is hard work—but also a blast. The proof: these fun pics from the various **ARROWVERSE SETS.** BY AMY WILKINSON

Red Steel

Star Grant Gustin flashes a rather serious look while filming the season 1 episode "Plastique." "I knew that it was big shoes to fill, being Barry Allen," he recalls of shooting his first few episodes of *The Flash*. "No matter what I'm doing, it's definitely about, 'How can I do the best job possible?'" Ah, superspeed *and* a work ethic!

Grin Arrow

Cast members David Ramsey, Emily Bett Rickards and Stephen Amell take a pause on the set of the 150th episode, "Emerald Archer"—a documentary-style hour narrated by Kelsey Grammer.

Directorial MVP

Kevin Smith (pictured here with *Supergirl* stars Nicole Maines, Melissa Benoist and Jesse Rath) has directed a number of *Supergirl* and *The Flash* episodes (and also cameoed on the latter). Recalls Gustin: "Kevin Smith cried the first time he saw me in the suit." Yes, really.

Midnight Train

Gustin, along with director Glen Winter and Wentworth Miller as Leonard Snart/Captain Cold, shoot a scene for "Going Rogue" on a railroad track. Miller would, of course, go on to star on his own Arrowverse show, *DC's Legends of Tomorrow*.

Tickling the Ivories

In the aptly titled *Flash-Supergirl* musical crossover "Duet," star Jeremy Jordan (previously of *Smash*) shows off his piano-playing skills. The song-and-dance hour also featured a cameo by *Glee* alum Darren Criss.

A First Time for Everything

The 2019 *Arrow* episode "Past Sins," marked star David Ramsey's directorial debut. Here he shoots a scene in the government research facility known as A.R.G.U.S.

The Man in Blue

Jesse L. Martin, who previous to starring as Det. Joe West on *The Flash* played Det. Ed Green on *Law & Order*, sits back on the set of 2016's "The Runaway Dinosaur." Even a cop needs a break now and then.

Comparing Notes
Arrow stars Echo Kellum and Ramsey review a script while filming 2019's "Emerald Archer."

Going Behind the Camera
Another Arrowverse star who's tried his hand at directing: *The Flash*'s Tom Cavanagh, who plays Harrison Wells on the CW series. He's pictured here on the set of season 3's "The Once and Future Flash," with costars Gustin and Carlos Valdes.

Center of Attention

Smith cracks Benoist up while directing the 2018 *Supergirl* episode "Bunker Hill." Benoist will make her own directorial debut this season. "I've been wanting to since season 3," she says.

ENTERTAINMENT WEEKLY
EDITOR JD Heyman
EXECUTIVE EDITOR & CREATIVE DIRECTOR Tim Leong
SENIOR ART DIRECTOR Faith Stafford

ARROWVERSE
EDITORIAL DIRECTOR Kostya Kennedy
EDITION EDITOR Alyssa Smith
EDITOR, PEOPLE + EW BOOKS Allison Adato
EDITOR Amy Wilkinson
DESIGNER Aaron Morales
PHOTO EDITOR Robert Conway
WRITERS Chancellor Agard, Breia Brissey, Samantha Highfill, Gina McIntyre, Rich Sands
REPORTER Daniel S. Levy
COPY DESK Joanann Scali (Chief), James Bradley (Deputy), Ellen Adamson, Gabrielle Danchick, Richard Donnelly, Ben Harte, Matt Weingarden
PRODUCTION DESIGNER Peter Niceberg
RESEARCH DIRECTOR Céline Wojtala
PREMEDIA TRAFFICKING SUPERVISOR Christopher Sprague
COLOR QUALITY ANALYST John Santucci

MEREDITH SPECIAL INTEREST MEDIA
VICE PRESIDENT & GROUP PUBLISHER Scott Mortimer
VICE PRESIDENT, GROUP EDITORIAL DIRECTOR Stephen Orr
VICE PRESIDENT, MARKETING Jeremy Biloon
EXECUTIVE ACCOUNT DIRECTOR Doug Stark
EXECUTIVE PUBLISHING DIRECTOR Megan Pearlman
DIRECTOR, BRAND MARKETING Jean Kennedy
SALES DIRECTOR Christi Crowley
ASSOCIATE DIRECTOR, BRAND MARKETING Bryan Christian
SENIOR BRAND MANAGER Katherine Barnet
ASSOCIATE DIRECTOR, BUSINESS DEVELOPMENT AND PARTNERSHIPS Nina Reed

EDITORIAL DIRECTOR Kostya Kennedy
CREATIVE DIRECTOR Gary Stewart
DIRECTOR OF PHOTOGRAPHY Christina Lieberman
EDITORIAL OPERATIONS DIRECTOR Jamie Roth Major
MANAGER, EDITORIAL OPERATIONS Gina Scauzillo

SPECIAL THANKS Brad Beatson, Melissa Frankenberry, Sandra Jurevics, Samantha Lebofsky, Emma H.P. Levy, Kate Roncinske, Laura Villano

MEREDITH NATIONAL MEDIA GROUP
PRESIDENT, MEREDITH MAGAZINES Doug Olson
PRESIDENT, CONSUMER PRODUCTS Tom Witschi
PRESIDENT, CHIEF DIGITAL OFFICER Catherine Levene
CHIEF REVENUE OFFICER Michael Brownstein
CHIEF MARKETING & DATA OFFICER Alysia Borsa
MARKETING & INTEGRATED COMMUNICATIONS Nancy Weber

SENIOR VICE PRESIDENTS
CONSUMER REVENUE Andy Wilson
CORPORATE SALES Brian Kightlinger
DIRECT MEDIA Patti Follo
RESEARCH SOLUTIONS Britta Cleveland
STRATEGIC SOURCING, NEWSSTAND, PRODUCTION Chuck Howell
DIGITAL SALES Marla Newman
THE FOUNDRY Matt Petersen
PRODUCT & TECHNOLOGY Justin Law

VICE PRESIDENTS
FINANCE Chris Susil
BUSINESS PLANNING & ANALYSIS Rob Silverstone
CONSUMER MARKETING Steve Crowe
SHOPPER MARKETING Carol Campbell
BRAND LICENSING Steve Grune

VICE PRESIDENT, GROUP EDITORIAL DIRECTOR Stephen Orr
DIRECTOR, EDITORIAL OPERATIONS & FINANCE Greg Kayko

MEREDITH CORPORATION
PRESIDENT & CHIEF EXECUTIVE OFFICER Tom Harty
CHIEF FINANCIAL OFFICER Joseph Ceryanec
CHIEF DEVELOPMENT OFFICER John Zieser
PRESIDENT, MEREDITH LOCAL MEDIA GROUP Patrick McCreery
SENIOR VICE PRESIDENT, HUMAN RESOURCES Dina Nathanson

CHAIRMAN Stephen M. Lacy
VICE CHAIRMAN Mell Meredith Frazier

meredith   MPA THE ASSOCIATION OF MAGAZINE MEDIA

For information on bulk purchases, please contact Suzanne Albert in the Special Sales Department at Suzanne.Albert@meredith.com.
Printed in the USA.

CREDITS
COVER Arrow: Diyah Pera/The CW; The Flash: Kharen Hill/The CW; Supergirl: Katie Yu/The CW; Batwoman: JSquared Photography/The CW; White Canary: The CW; **BACK COVER** Felicity Smoak, The Atom: Shane Harvey/The CW (2); Black Lightning: Mark Hill/The CW; Dinah Drake: Marc Hom/The CW; Vibe, John Constantine: Jack Rowand/The CW (2); **Pg 1** Art Streiber/August; **Pg 2-3** Art Streiber/August; **Pg 6-7** Bettina Strauss/The CW; heads from top: Bob Mahoney/The CW; Katie Yu/The CW; Robert Falconer/The CW; **Pg 8-9** heads from top: Warner Bros.; Bettmann/Getty Images; Jeffrey Thurnher; David Gray; David James/Warner Bros.; clockwise: Parrish Lewis/The CW; Katie Yu/The CW; Jack Rowand/The CW; Bettina Strauss/The CW; **Pg 10-11** from left: DC; Katie Yu/The CW; Christopher Patey/Contour by Getty Images; **Pg 12-13** clockwise from top left: Cate Cameron/The CW; Bettina Strauss/The CW; Jack Rowand/The CW(3); Dean Buscher/The CW; **Pg 14-15** clockwise from left: Annette Brown/The CW; Eliza Morse/The CW; Bob Mahoney/The CW; Annette Brown/The CW; **Pg 18-19** clockwise from left: Bettina Strauss/The CW; Jack Rowand/The CW; Cate Cameron/The CW (2); heads from top: Frank Ockenfels III/The CW; Dean Buscher/The CW; Diyah Pera/The CW; Mathieu Young/The CW; **Pg 20-21** heads from top: Daniel Power/The CW; Mathieu Young/The CW; Jack Rowand/The CW; Cate Cameron/The CW; Katie Yu/The CW; clockwise from left: Jack Rowand/The CW; Cate Cameron/The CW (3); **Pg 23** from top: Dean Buscher/The CW; Katie Yu/The CW; heads from top: Cate Cameron/The CW; Dean Buscher/The CW; Cate Cameron/The CW; Dean Buscher/The CW; Diyah Pera/The CW; Matthew Simmons/FilmMagic; **Pg 24-25** heads from top: Shane Harvey/The CW; Cate Cameron/The CW; Bettina Strauss/The CW; Jack Rowand/The CW; Robert Falconer/The CW; clockwise from left: Jack Rowand/The CW; Diyah Pera/The CW; Jack Rowand/The CW; **Pg 26** heads from top: Dean Buscher/The CW (2); Katie Yu/The CW; Jack Rowand/The CW; David Livingston/Getty Images; from top: Dean Buscher/The CW; Jack Rowand/The CW; **Pg 27** top row from l-r: Jack Rowand/The CW; Dean Buscher/The CW; second row l-r: Diyah Pera/The CW; Daniel Power/The CW; Jack Rowand/The CW; third row l-r: Cate Cameron/The CW; Dean Buscher/The CW; Katie Yu/The CW; Diyah Pera/The CW; fourth row l-r: Jack Rowand/The CW (2); Cate Cameron/The CW; Michael Courtney/The CW; **Pg 30** Jack Rowand/The CW; **Pg 31** Ben Watts; **Pg 32-33** clockwise from left: Jack Rowand/The CW; Diyah Pera/The CW; Dan Power/The CW; **Pg 36-37** clockwise: Diyah Pera/The CW; Cate Cameron/The CW (2); heads from top: Frank Ockenfels III/The CW; Diyah Pera/The CW; Nino Munoz/The CW; Katie Yu/The CW; **Pg 38** heads from top: Kharen Hill/The CW; Katie Yu/The CW; Jack Rowand/The CW; Cate Cameron/The CW; Katie Yu/The CW (2); from top: Diyah Pera/The CW; Katie Yu/The CW; **Pg 40-41** clockwise from top left: Katie Yu/The CW; The CW; Katie Yu/The CW; Jack Rowand/The CW; heads from top: Katie Yu/The CW; Shane Harvey/The CW; Katie Yu/The CW (3); Sergei Bachlakov/The CW; Diyah Pera/The CW; **Pg 44-45** from left: Cate Cameron/The CW; Robert Falconer/The CW; Andrew H Walker/Variety/Shutterstock; **Pg 50-51** clockwise: Robert Voets/Warner Bros./CBS; Diyah Pera/The CW; Bettina Strauss/The CW; heads from top: Matthias Clamer/CBS; Robert Falconer/The CW; Dean Buscher/The CW; Bettina Strauss/The CW; **Pg 52** heads from top: Robert Falconer/The CW; Bettina Strauss/The CW; Dean Buscher/The CW; Katie Yu/The CW; Diyah Pera/The CW (2); from top: Robert Falconer/The CW; Dean Buscher/The CW; **Pg 54-55** clockwise: Jeff Weddell/The CW; Sergie Bachlakov/The CW; Robert Falconer/The CW; heads from top: Diyah Pera/The CW; Robert Falconer/The CW; Diyah Pera/The CW (2); Colin Bentley/The CW; Sergei Bachlakov/The CW; **Pg 58** Diyah Pera/The CW; **Pg 64-65** clockwise: Dean Buscher/The CW; Diyah Pera/The CW; Jeff Weddell/The CW; Dean Buscher/The CW; heads from top: Diyah Pera/The CW; Katie Yu/The CW; Shane Harvey/The CW; Diyah Pera/The CW; Bettina Strauss/The CW; **Pg 67** clockwise: Dean Buscher/The CW; Robert Falconer/The CW; Bettina Strauss/The CW; heads from top: Diyah Pera/The CW; Jordon Nuttall/The CW; Cate Cameron/The CW; Jordon Nuttall/The CW; Katie Yu/The CW; Dean Buscher/The CW; Bettina Strauss/The CW; **Pg 68-69** heads from top: Dean Buscher/The CW; Jack Rowand/The CW; Katie Yu/The CW; Cate Cameron/The CW; Jack Rowand/The CW; Dean Buscher/The CW; clockwise: Dean Buscher/The CW; Jack Rowand/The CW; Dean Buscher/The CW; **Pg 70-71** Andrew H Walker/Variety/Shutterstock; **Pg 72** Robert Falconer/The CW; **Pg 73** Michael Buckner/TVLine/Shutterstock; **Pg 74-75** Andre H Walker/Variety/Shutterstock (4); **Pg 76** Katie Yu/The CW; **Pg 77** Michael Buckner/TVLine/Shutterstock; **Pg 82-83** clockwise: Kimberly French/The CW (3); heads from top: Kimberly French/The CW; Jordon Nuttall/The CW (2); **Pg 85** Kimberly French/The CW (3) heads: Jordon Nuttall/The CW (4); **Pg 88** from top: JSquared Photography/Contour by Getty Images; Kimberly French/The CW **Pg 90-91** clockwise: Jack Rowand/The CW; Shane Harvey/The CW; Sergei Bachlakov/The CW; **Pg 92-93** Cate Cameron/The CW; Jack Rowand/The CW; Katie Yu/The CW; Jack Rowand/The CW; **Pg 94-95** clockwise: Katie Yu/The CW; Shane Harvey/The CW; Sergei Bachlakov/The CW; **Pg 96** Art Streiber/August

"I'M SO PROUD OF GRANT AND MELISSA AND HOW CAITY HAS GROWN INTO THE LEADER THAT SHE IS. I'M PUMPED FOR RUBY"

—STEPHEN AMELL ON HIS COSTARS